Innovation Intermediaries and (Final) Frontiers of High-tech

Matjaz Vidmar

Innovation Intermediaries and (Final) Frontiers of High-tech

Supporting the New Space Sector in Scotland

palgrave
macmillan

Matjaz Vidmar
Institute for the Study of Science, Technology and Innovation
The University of Edinburgh, Royal Observatory Edinburgh
Blackford Hill, Edinburgh, UK

ISBN 978-3-030-60641-1 ISBN 978-3-030-60642-8 (eBook)
https://doi.org/10.1007/978-3-030-60642-8

This Palgrave Macmillan imprint is published by the registered company Springer Nature Switzerland AG.
The registered company address is: Gewerbestrasse 11, 6330 Cham, Switzerland

To those who I hope will find it useful—
and to you who made it all possible.

Acknowledgements

This book is based in part on my doctoral thesis *Scottish Space Sector and Innovation: A PERIpatetic study of an emerging innovation system and the roles of innovation intermediaries* (Vidmar 2019a). In addition, some of the core premises of this monograph were presented as part of DRUID 2018 conference in Copenhagen (June 2018). Some of the material was also presented and separately published in two journal articles: the landscape mapping and typology of intermediaries roles were part of *Proceedings of the 70th International Astronautical Congress* in Washington (October 2019) and published in *Acta Astronautica* (Vidmar 2021); and the comparative cases of Higgs Centre for Innovation and Space-SI were presented at the *smartEIZ* conference in Zagreb (October 2018) and published in *Croatian Economic Survey* (Vidmar 2019b).

None of this work would be possible without the support and guidance of my doctoral supervisors at the University of Edinburgh: Alessandro Roseillo, Niki Vermeulen and Robin Williams; and my mentor at the Science and Technology Facilities Council, Julian Dines. Additional thanks go to Tim Vorley, who led my Innovation Caucus internship, where some of the key premises of this work were developed, and Franc Mali, who hosted and guided me when researching Slovenian Space Sector, including the study of Space-SI. I would further like to thank a plethora of colleagues from across the University of Edinburgh who provided advice and feedback on ideas presented in this book, especially Jamie Fleck.

Keeping an eye on the quality of my work, I thank the editors and anonymous reviewers of the book and the papers I have submitted to conferences and for journal publications. I would particularly like to mention here Ken Davidian and Zoran Aralica, whose both encouragement and criticism were instrumental in the improvement of the style and substance of my work. I further thank the amazing team at Palgrave, my saintly patient and supportive commissioning editor, Rachael Ballard, and equally dedicated and encouraging production editor, Joanna O'Niell. Your tolerance of my excuses for delays as well as your genuine interest in my work made this new adventure enjoyable, exciting and manageable (even amidst of the Spring 2020 Covid-19 pandemic).

Most importantly, this research would not be possible without all of my informants, the fifty or so amazing individuals who took the time to assist me in my enquiries through any of the formal data collection exercises, as well as several hundred others, with whom I spoke informally about my work. I am neither able nor allowed to share all your names here, but you may rest assured that I will never forget the help and insight provided by any single one of you.

Finally, the unwavering support from my family and friends has been my rock through all the challenges and successes of this project. Words cannot express my love and admiration for my partner, Julija, who has shown infinite patience in the face of my increasingly obsessive relationship with this work. My mum, Vesna, has been my greatest supporter and my best critic. The numerous little ways in which my friends and colleagues at Edinburgh and around the world have kept me safe and sound, and have given me love and support, make me feel truly humbled and blessed.

This research has only been possible through the generous studentship from the SGSSS Doctoral Training Partnership, funded by the Economic and Social Research Council (ESRC; grant number ES/J500136/1); the SGSSS Overseas Institutional Visit (OIV) Grant; Innovate UK—ESRC 2017 Innovation Caucus internship [funded through ESRC grant number ES/T000570/1]; numerous other small grants and awards (William Dickson Traveling Fund, IAF Emerging Space Leaders Award, ESA International Space Education Board Scholarship, SGAC European Space Leader Award, STIS Travel Funding and Graduate School Office Practice Programme grants); and in-kind support from STFC/ATC Innovations team. Substantial development on this book was done as part of two great writing retreats: the SKAPE retreat to Peebles Hydro (June 2019) and the PF-STIS retreat to Gargunnock House (November 2019).

References

Vidmar, M. (2019a). *Scottish Space Sector and Innovation a PERIpatetic Study of an Emerging Innovation System and the Roles of Innovation Intermediaries.* Edinburgh: The University of Edinburgh.

Vidmar, M. (2019b). The Ten Million Euro Question: How Do Innovation Intermediaries Support Smart Specialization? *Croatian Economic Survey, 21*, 37–84.

Vidmar, M. (2021). Enablers, Equippers, Shapers and Movers: A Typology of innovation intermediaries interventions and the development of an emergent innovation system. *Acta Astronautica, 179*, 280–289.

Contents

List of Figures

List of Tables

CHAPTER 1

Introduction

Abstract This chapter outlines the critical importance of innovation intermediation with reference to macro-level new industrial and innovation policy, chiefly smart specialisation, and micro-level technology development management. Presenting the particular challenges of the emergence of new high-tech sectors, in particular the empirical case study, the New Space sector in Scotland.

Keywords Economic development • High-tech industries • Innovation intermediaries • Geographically-Bound Sectoral Systems of Innovation • New Space sector

As a response to globalisation of core manufacturing industries, and in particular their migration to emerging industrial countries in Asia, Western economic development policy has moved towards investment in specialised, high-added value technological products. Policy formulation focused on extending and exploiting geo-political and economic strengths and aimed to suport discrete industrial sectors, which can develop and retain global competitive advantage. In particular, variants of new industrial and innovation policy agenda (Radosevic 2017) have emerged as leading the way in this new agenda. These policy frameworks rejected both the principles of an absentee government in free-market economic deregulation of

M. Vidmar, *Innovation Intermediaries and (Final) Frontiers of High-tech*, https://doi.org/10.1007/978-3-030-60642-8_1

the turn of the twenty-first century as well as the doctrines of industrial planning of the post-Second-World-War era. The emerging policy compromise was in the middle of the said spectrum—government-set priorities with free-market implementation. This gave rise to policymakers developing and deploying at-arms-length instruments and organisations in support of multi-party industrial development—in particular through innovation intermediaries.

Though many of the policy instruments are seen as ways of addressing perceived market failure (Arrow 1951) or government failure (Tullock et al. 2002), arguably policy can be more proactive in establishing economic opportunities where there has been none before (Mazzucato and Penna 2016). Perhaps the most well-known of such policy frameworks is the European Union's Smart Specialisation Strategy (S3) (European Commission 2014). S3 has by and large now been superseded by national innovation programmes and industrial strategies, however, under the surface these are actually very similar instruments. In an increasingly knowledge-based global economic system, these policies tend to focus on establishing and supporting industrial sectors with high productivity. High added-value products and services are particularly desirable as they increase countries' GDPs, as well as subsequent tax returns and develop global competitiveness. Hence, the policies strive to align the strengths of the scientific and technical knowledge base with the context of market formation using macro- and micro-economic instruments, supporting reindustrialisation (Stojčić and Aralica 2018) and encouraging trade.

The critical underpinnings of such policies are, on the one hand, a rise in support for bottom-up development from start-up and spin-off companies and, on the other hand, an increase in openness innovation process as a guarantee of the competitive advantage on the global stage. A lot of the focus of economic and industrial development has thus shifted away from large corporations, sometimes labelled as "national primes", and towards small- and medium-sized enterprises (SMEs). This corresponds to the increasing recognition of entrepreneurial and research and development (R&D) drivers for economic activities (Neffke et al. 2014; Wright et al. 2015). Knowledge-intensive technological entrepreneurship has been found to be particularly critical and a significant target for policymakers (Malerba et al. 2015; Thérin 2007). In particular, it is argued that a paradigm shift occurred through the conceptualisation of Open Innovation, that is the notion that innovation processes cross-organisational/firm boundaries (Chesbrough 2003).

The dynamics of Open Innovation is closely related to the innovation systems (IS) approach of understanding the consolidated capacity for innovation (Cooke 2001; Freeman 1991; Hekkert et al. 2007; Malerba 2002). Innovation systems analysis provides a comprehensive conceptualisation of the systemic nature of innovation, framed as an inter-organisational and context-dependent activity. The boundaries of such systems can be defined in different ways, though a combination of sectoral/technological and geographical considerations has been proposed as optimal (Edquist 2004). This has not always been taken up as consistently, and the innovation systems literature has split to examine either geographical (Cooke 2001; Nelson 1993) or sectoral/technological dynamics (Bergek et al. 2008; Breschi and Malerba 1997). However, a combined approach has been de-facto used in many studies, in particular in the field of innovation intermediation. This is likely due to geo-sectoral boundaries being helpful to study the complex landscape of innovation activities by stabilising the research within a relatively homogeneous environment of a shared knowledge base as well as exogenious factors (politics, economics, demographics, etc.). This framing can be acknowledged explicitly, by contextualising systemic innovation research as situated in Geographically-Bound Sectoral Systems of Innovation (GSSI), as argued in this book and elsewhere (Vidmar et al. 2020).

However, there persists an acute lack of integration of the three key elements of understanding and supporting innovation: current micro-level literature on innovation process (Swann 2009); the meso-level literature on regional and sectoral innovation systems (Freeman 1991); and capacity building within the macro-level innovation policy context (Flanagan et al. 2011). In particular, this concerns the pathways linking micro-level organisational behaviours or firms and other actors, meso-level inter-organisational interaction between them and macro-level policy interventions and support (Chesbrough and Bogers 2014; Lee et al. 2010; West et al. 2014). The particular emerging concern is the notion of transition towards Open Innovation, that is: how do SMEs adopt/change their innovation processes and organisational behaviour to succeed in this more open environment? Furthermore, how are these new opportunities translated from meso- (inter-organisational) to micro- (firm) level and how are they built upon or influenced on a systemic level, that is meso- to macro- and the reverse?

These questions are especially pertinent as SMEs became the focus of innovation policy in many countries, including the UK, as mentioned previously (Bodas Freitas and von Tunzelmann 2008; Chesbrough and Vanhaverbeke 2011; Cooke 2012; Doh and Kim 2014; Love and Roper 2015). Furthermore, lack of integrated analytical perspectives in innovation studies hinder the development of coherent theory to allow a more consistent understanding of the actors and their actions within the dynamically evolving business ecosystem (Tsujimoto et al. 2018). However, before any of the above substantive questions are answered, we have to establish what are the boundaries of the study of innovation intermediation?

Unit of Analysis: Geographically-Bound Sectoral Systems of Innovation

Scholarly interest in innovation and the economic role it plays is often traced back to Schumpeter's seminal work on entrepreneurship and wealth creation (Malerba and Orsenigo 1995). Subsequent research can be divided into two main branches: examinations of the micro-level role of innovation in a firm and its relation to development and growth; and studies of macro-level economic and social theory, examining the effect of innovation on the economy and society as a whole (Pavitt 2003; Swann 2009). Most recently, a very successful paradigm for macro-level studies was created, namely the innovation systems (IS) framework (Freeman 1991). This encapsulates most of the macro-level effects and has been adapted to studies of various scales and purposes.

The main gist of the IS theory is that innovation should be understood as an interaction between (groups of) actors, their capacities, activities and structural norms that govern their behaviour. Specifically, it has been shown that the innovation systems model can be framed using geographical boundaries, such as the national level (Freeman 1991; Georghiou 1993; Lundvall et al. 2002; Nelson 1993) or the regional level (Asheim et al. 2011; Cooke 2001; Cooke et al. 1997). Alternatively, the model can be applied according to areas of economic activity, utilising either technological (Bergek et al. 2008; Hekkert et al. 2007) or sectoral (Malerba 2002, 2004, 2005) platforms. However, these different levels of enquiry share the same common framework of the innovation systems model, tailored according to the scope and aims of different researchers' interests (Frenz and Oughton 2005). For example:

> *Edquist (2004) has argued that system boundaries may be defined in one of three ways: spatially/geographically; sectorally; and in terms of system activities or functions.* (Asheim et al. 2011)

In contrast, this book argues that for detailed and complete micro-level studies of innovation systems, most authors de-facto adopt all three sets of boundaries to define the studied environment and roles of the various actors/players within them.

A detailed literature review was carried out using the Scopus database. The "innovation intermediary" search term returns 161 documents, of which 108 were journal papers. Given this study's interest in innovation systems approach, it was established that about three-quarters of those publications, 131 (89 journal articles), also contain the key phrase "innovation system" and 104 (68) also contain the key phrase "open innovation". Of all papers initially identified, forty-two were deemed relevant for this review, based on the title, abstract analysis and availability to read and download via the University of Edinburgh library services. Further analysis yielded only a handful of studies, which are presented in this monograph, focusing on systemic roles and containing more than one single case study and/or a single intermediary function/role, hence, giving insights relevant for systemic classification framework, which is the aim of this study. Finally, seven systemic reviews were identified as core to the analysis of past classifications (Dalziel 2010; Howells 2006; Kilelu et al. 2011; Kim 2015; Kivimaa 2014; Lukkarinen et al. 2018; Nilsson and Sia-Ljungström 2013).

When analysing recent empirical studies looking at innovation intermediaries within innovation systems (see Table 1.1), key emerging themes included an overwhelming focus on knowledge and technology brokerage and recent interest in crowdsourcing and digital intermediary platforms. However, the latter's systemic role and value are harder to characterise owing to novelty and somewhat selective applicability, as they more often than not concern themselves with exclusive knowledge and technology transfer and workforce upskilling. However, these are likely to become more prominent in the future, particularly in the current (post-)Covid-19 context. In particular, noting the fast pace of the spread of digital technologies and growing importance of activities' coordination in entrepreneurial context, the availability of relevant knowledge in the innovation system (Malerba and McKelvey 2020) will likley be a necessary condition for the success of innovation intermediaries in the near future.

Table 1.1 Brief summary of some of the key empirical studies of innovation intermediaries since 2010, indicating the three defining boundaries: geography, sector and function(s)

Study	*Geography*	*Sector*	*Function(s)*
Lukkarinen et al. (2018)	Finland	Cleantech	Alignment of interests, the building of capacities and the formation of markets
Lin, Zeng, Liu, and Li (2016)	China	Manufacturing	Absorptive capacity
Mgumia, Mattee, and Kundi (2015)	Tanzania	Agriculture	Demand articulation, network brokerage and innovation process management
Iturrioz, Aragón, and Narvaiza (2015)	Spain	Modragon cooperative	Social capital
Kivimaa (2014)	Finland	Energy	Political positions and roles of intermediaries in transitions
Nilsson and Sia-Ljungström (2013)	Sweden and Denmark	Food	Regional Innovation System Development
Agogué, Ystrom, and Le Masson (2013)	France and Sweden	Traffic safety engineering	Structuring collective exploration
Hargreaves, Hielscher, Seyfang, and Smith (2012)	UK	Community energy	Niche development
Klewitz, Zeyen, and G Hansen (2013)	Germany	Metal and mechanical engineering	Sustainability transition
Boon, Moors, Kuhlmann, and Smits (2011)	Netherlands	Health care sector	Demand articulation
Kilelu et al. (2011)	Kenya	Agriculture	Innovation brokering

In addition, a key observation is that most studies take a sectoral focus while also having a clearly defined geographical boundary. For instance, Nilsson and Sia-Ljungström note this approach as "sector-specific regional innovation systems" (Nilsson and Sia-Ljungström 2013, p. 161). Such detailed framing is also apparent in some policy contributions (Bendis et al. 2008). Though recent empirical work on innovation intermediation on the basis of platforms transcends this compartmentalisation (Hossain

2017; Kokshagina and Masson 2015), they focus more on processes behind the operation of platform-based intermediation than on their effects as interventions in innovation systems supporting open innovation.

Hence, through empirical practice and theoretical consideration, a new de facto framing has emerged—Geographically-Bound Sectoral Systems of Innovation (GSSI)—which is the most accessible, comprehensive and homogeneous unit of analysis. The GSSI's constituent actors share the same economic, political and social environment, whilst also supporting the required diversity and complexity to analyse both generic (systemic) interventions and sector-specific ones. Sectoral emergence dynamics, sustainability and digital transitions, and systemic differences between sectors and/or geographies can also be very effectively exposed by this framing, as it can be used in empirical studies to compare case studies between places, before and after timelines and contrast different sectors.

In addition to GSSI grounding, the functionalist boundaries of the examined review studies present a critical challenge to the innovation intermediaries literature, as they are very varied and do not easily fit a single comprehensive systematisation of all deployed roles and functions. Most of the studies examined focus predominantly on the networking and brokerage functions and facilities within the GSSI framing, and are not proposing to develop a more generalisable model of intermediation. This leads to a lack of clarity amongst practitioners and scholars alike as to what innovation intermediaries as a whole are or can be (Abbate et al. 2013; Dalziel 2010; Hannon et al. 2014; Howells 2006; Van der Meulen et al. 2005). Hence, in order to develop a more comprehensive model of innovation intermediaries activities and roles, a thorough look at their core definition is necessary.

Innovation Intermediaries

The innovation intermediary label has been used to group together a varied set of organisations. It includes multi-party intermediaries, such as knowledge brokers, as well as service providers, for example, business incubators and accelerators. In short, innovation intermediaries are often a shorthand for any organisation involved in an innovation process as long as they do not directly benefit from the developed product or service. This is examined in more detail in next chapter and a new functional definition proposed. A lot of interest has been expressed in understanding the systemic role of intermediaries in supporting innovation processes (Dosi et al. 2006; Duff 1996; Green et al. 1999; Ngwenya and Hagmann 2011; Smits and Kuhlmann 2004). In addition, a significant body of literature has emerged about innovation intermediation with specific reference to Open Innovation (Antikaninen et al. 2009; Chesbrough 2006; Katzy et al. 2013; Kokshagina and Masson 2015) and innovation systems (Kerry and Danson 2016; Klerkx et al. 2015; Nilsson and Sia-Ljungström 2013).

Just looking at definitions of innovation intermediaries, a substantial focus on knowledge brokerage can be found in the literature (Kilelu et al. 2011), while separate studies have also analysed a variety of other roles intermediaries play in innovation systems, such as business incubation and network development. This has led to the concern that although the innovation intermediaries literature is well established, it is, as explicitly noted by many authors, currently too fragmented and limited in understanding of available interventions (Abbate et al. 2013; Dalziel 2010; Hannon et al. 2014; Howells 2006; Van der Meulen et al. 2005).

Though many attempts at systematising the extensive empirical studies of intermediaries' activities and roles were made (Dalziel 2010; Kilelu et al. 2011; Kim 2015; Kivimaa 2014; Klerkx et al. 2015; Lukkarinen et al. 2018), feedback from both scholars and practitioners indicates a continued lack of clarity and operational applicability. While these studies all aimed to bring different approaches to the study and development of innovation intermediaries closer together, the dividing lines between intermediaries' supply of resources versus engaging in direct activities, close involvement versus systemic provision and providing physical interventions versus deploying social capital were seldom crossed—as is explored later in this volume. Hence, most of the emerging classifications and typologies were incomplete and their operationalisation in practice hindered by an acute lack of clarity.

This is a particularly persistent challenge evident in addressing more programmatic and normative questions, such as: what should an intermediary do to achieve a certain result in a given context? Similarly, scholars often struggle to ascribe specific systemic roles to individual intermediaries, as their engagement in a targeted economic unit (in most cases a geographically-bound sector) seems either too scattered or too unspecific/broad (Hannon et al. 2014). While addressing this challenge is very context specific (Martin and Scott 2000) - depending on the sector and the (geographical) placing - high-tech sectors do bear some cross-disciplinary similarities allowing for generalisable best practice. In this book, the emergence of the New Space sector in previously peripheral countries for Space

Industry has served as the perfect empirical test-bed to explore the state of the art and develop new theoretical and practical tools to better understand innovation intermediation.

Final Frontier(s): New Space Sector Transition, Scotland and Innovation Intermediation

Many studies have called for the development of better specific and general understanding of innovation intermediaries activities. For instance, Venturini and Verbano (2014) mention several understudied aspects of technology transfer and innovation intermediation in the Space Industry, advocating for an:

> *Analysis of the intervention of brokers (including private) and other organizations devoted to facilitate the transfer such as incubators, venture capital companies, science and technology parks.* (Venturini and Verbano 2014, p. 109)

This is particularly timely since global Space Industry is currently in transition to New Space—that is smaller and cheaper hardware and more easily accessible space data (Adlen 2011)—which is expanding space-related economic activity into new, previously peripheral geographical areas. This paradigm shift has been particularly successful in establishing a budding ecosystem of New Space SMEs in Scotland, which is sometimes referred to as the Space Glen. Interestingly, analysis of this development (Vidmar 2020) points to it being linked to the UK and Scottish policymakers addressing the growth of the New Space sector within the innovation policy, rather than through a separate space policy programme. The resulting small-scale and dispersed investment in R&D and business development put forward by the various governmental and private actors led to the creation of dispersed and divergent clusters of firms, strongly linked to research expertise at local universities, as well as to other sectors with more mature markets, such as oil and gas and forestry. Since 2010, these are being joined together in a common regional sectoral identity, via industry-led grouping initiatives mainly through promotion at events. This grouping also led to the development of a more collaborative/open innovation process involving multiple parties, and an industry with a loosely consolidated value chain, which is referred to as Agile Space and operates as a living laboratory (Vidmar 2019). Critically, the sector seems to be joined together by the innovation intermediaries, as they are found at the core of innovation networks steering processes of organisational learning (Vidmar et al. 2020).

As such, the emerging Scottish New Space sector is a perfect case study to examine innovation intermediaries, their activities, strategies, roles and impacts within a high-tech economic development context, within the GSSI framing. In fact, the Space Industry has been often considered as the "final frontier" of techno-scientific advancement (Genta and Rycroft 2003). The geographical boundary of Scotland is advantageous, as its territorial size and socio-economic and political characteristics make it a very well-proportioned and coherent empirical sample. Sectorally, high-tech SMEs within the Space Industry are both developing along an emerging geographical specialisation, as well as aligning to a global transition within the context of the New Space sector. Temporally, the empirical research is situated between 2014 and 2017, with data collected on events going as far back as early as the 2000s. During this time the transition in Scotland was at its mid-point—there was an almost equal number of pre-New Space players as the emerging New Space ones—enabling maximum exposure to the multiple dynamics that innovation intermediaries were involved with/subjected to.

Examining the policy aspects of the sectoral development, the role of innovation intermediaries was noted as crucial, in particular as the governmental policy to develop this sector is based on delivering dispersed interventions in supporting innovation, rather than a unified national programme (Vidmar 2020). Additional insight into the importance of these innovation intermediaries comes from understanding the critical role the innovation intermediaries play in this ecosystem, as expressed by the key firms involved in its activities. Overall, the Scottish New Space sector seems a perfect case study to test the development of a new model for understanding and deploying innovation intermediation support in an emerging high-tech sector.

Book Outline

This book first examines the evolving definition of innovation intermediaries and its shortcomings of past attempts of their classification (Chap. 2). Secondly, presenting the empirical case study of the innovation intermediation landscape of the emerging New Space sector in Scotland (Chap. 3), it re-enforces the need for a more holistic understanding of the various combinations of roles and activities innovation intermediaries have and undertake. Thirdly it goes on to propose a new classification of innovation intermediaries' interventions, outlines their contextual factors and proposes a typology of innovation intermediaries' roles (Chap. 4), bringing together the state of the art in the literature by examining the dividing lines. Fourthly, it deploys this new model in the main empirical study—New Space sector in Scotland—as well as exploring further the organisational configuration of innovation intermediaries and the relationship between policy and operational deployment of interventions and fulfilment of (eco)systemic roles (Chap. 5). Lastly, a set of tools is presented for policymakers, innovation intermediaries' managers, and research and business stakeholders, based on a series of past projects and contexts (Chap. 6). These tools can be used for the development of geo-sectoral economic development policy, innovation intermediaries' intervention programmes and offer reflections on wider ecosystems.

Bibliography

Abbate, T., Coppolino, R., & Schiavone, F. (2013). Linking Entities in Knowledge Transfer: The Innovation Intermediaries. *Journal of the Knowledge Economy, 4*, 233–243. https://doi.org/10.1007/s13132-013-0156-5.

Adlen, S. (2011). *Innovation in the Global Space Industry*. London: Imperial College London.

Agogué, M., Ystrom, A., & Le Masson, P. (2013). Rethinking the Role of Intermediaries as an Architect of Collective Exploration and Creation of Knowledge in Open Innovation. *International Journal of Innovation Management, 17*, 1350007. https://doi.org/10.1142/S1363919613500072.

Antikaninen, M., Mäkipää, M., & Ahonen, M. (2009). Motivating and Supporting Collaboration in Open Innovation. *Technology Management, 13*, 24.

Arrow, K. J. (1951). An Extension of the Basic Theorems of Classical Welfare Economics. In *Proceedings of the Second Berkeley Symposium on Mathematical Statistics and Probability* (pp. 507–532). Berkley: University of California.

Asheim, B. T., Smith, H. L., & Oughton, C. (2011). Regional Innovation Systems: Theory, Empirics and Policy. *Regional Studies, 45*, 875–891. https://doi.org/10.1080/00343404.2011.596701.

Bendis, R. A., Seline, R. S., & Byler, E. J. (2008). A New Direction for Technology-Based Economic Development: The Role of Innovation Intermediaries. *Industry and Higher Education, 22*, 73–80. https://doi.org/10.5367/000000008784139460.

Bergek, A., Jacobsson, S., Carlsson, B., Lindmark, S., & Rickne, A. (2008). Analyzing the Functional Dynamics of Technological Innovation Systems: A Scheme of Analysis. *Research Policy, 37*, 407–429. https://doi.org/10.1016/j.respol.2007.12.003.

Bodas Freitas, I. M., & von Tunzelmann, N. (2008). Mapping Public Support for Innovation: A Comparison of Policy Alignment in the UK and France. *Research Policy, 37*, 1446–1464. https://doi.org/10.1016/J.RESPOL.2008.05.005.

Boon, W. P., Moors, E. H., Kuhlmann, S., & Smits, R. E. (2011). Demand Articulation in Emerging Technologies: Intermediary User Organisations as Co-Producers? *Research Policy, 40*, 242–252.

Breschi, S., & Malerba, F. (1997). Sectoral Innovation Systems: Technological Regimes, Schumpeterian Dynamics, and Spatial Boundaries. In C. Edquist (Ed.), *Systems of Innovation: Technologies, Institutions and Organizations* (pp. 130–156). Abingdon: Routledge.

Chesbrough, H. (2003). *Open Innovation: The New Imperative for Creating and Profiting from Technology*. Boston: Harvard Business School Press.

Chesbrough, H. (2006). Innovation Intermediaries Enabling Open innovation. In *Open Business Models: How to Thrive in the New Innovation Landscape* (p. 33). https://doi.org/10.1107/S1600536808017583.

Chesbrough, H., & Bogers, M. (2014). *Explicating Open Innovation: Clarifying an Emerging Paradigm for Understanding Innovation, New Frontiers in Open Innovation*. Oxford: Oxford University Press. https://doi.org/10.1093/acprof.

Chesbrough, H., & Vanhaverbeke, W. (2011). *Open Innovation and Public Policy in Europe*. Research Report. https://doi.org/10.2873/886211.

Cooke, P. (2001). Regional Innovation Systems, Clusters, and the Knowledge Economy. *Industrial and Corporate Change, 10*, 945–974. https://doi.org/10.1093/icc/10.4.945.

Cooke, P. (2012). Knowledge Economy Spillovers, Proximity, and Specialization. In *Interactive Learning for Innovation* (pp. 100–111). London: Palgrave Macmillan. https://doi.org/10.1057/9780230362420_5.

Cooke, P., Gomez Uranga, M., & Etxebarria, G. (1997). Regional Innovation Systems: Institutional and Organisational Dimensions. *Research Policy, 26*, 475–491. https://doi.org/10.1016/S0048-7333(97)00025-5.

Dalziel, M. (2010). Why Do Innovation Intermediaries Exist? In *Druid 2010: Opening Up Innovation: Strategy, Organization and Technology* (p. 23). London: Imperial College London Business School.

Doh, S., & Kim, B. (2014). Government Support for SME Innovations in the Regional Industries: The Case of Government Financial Support Program in South Korea. *Research Policy, 43*, 1557–1569. https://doi.org/10.1016/J.RESPOL.2014.05.001.

Dosi, G., Malerba, F., Ramello, G. B., & Silva, F. (2006). Information, Appropriability, and the Generation of Innovative Knowledge Four Decades After Arrow and Nelson: An Introduction. *Industrial and Corporate Change, 15*, 891–901. https://doi.org/10.1093/icc/dtl028.

Duff, A. (1996). Best Practice in Business Incubator Management. [Report]. Booragoon: AUSTEP Strategic Partnering.

Edquist, C. (2004). Reflections on the Systems of Innovation Approach. *Science and Public Policy, 31*, 485–489.

European Commission. (2014). *Regional Research and Innovation Strategies for Smart Specialisation (RIS3)*. Brussels.

Flanagan, K., Uyarra, E., & Laranja, M. (2011). Reconceptualising the 'Policy Mix' for Innovation. *Research Policy, 40*, 702–713. https://doi.org/10.1016/j.respol.2011.02.005.

Freeman, C. (1991). Networks of Innovators: A Synthesis of Research Issues. *Research Policy, 20*, 499–514. https://doi.org/10.1016/0048-7333(91)90072-X.

Frenz, M., & Oughton, C. (2005). Innovation in the UK Regions and Devolved Administrations: A Review of the Literature. In *Final Report for the Department of Trade and ....* London: Department for Trade and Industry.

Genta, G., & Rycroft, M. (2003). *Space, the Final Frontier?* Cambridge: Cambridge University Press.

Georghiou, L. (1993). National Systems of Innovation. In B.-A. Lundvall (Ed.), *Towards a Theory of Innovation and Interactive Learning* (Pinter Publishers, London. 1992, pp. xiii + 342, £45, ISBN 1-85567-063-1, Prometheus). London: Pinter. https://doi.org/10.1080/08109029308629360.

Green, K., Hull, R., Mcmeekin, A., & Walsh, V. (1999). The Construction of the Techno-Economic: Networks Vs. Paradigms. *Research Policy, 28*, 777–792.

Hannon, M. J., Skea, J., & Rhodes, A. (2014). Facilitating and Coordinating UK Energy Innovation Through Systemic Innovation Intermediaries. In *International Conference on Sustainability Transitions* (pp. 27–29). https://www.imperial.ac.uk/media/imperial-college/research-centres-and-groups/rcuk-energy-strategy-fellowship/public/Hannon-2014-Systemic-Innovation-Intermediaries.pdf

Hargreaves, T., Hielscher, S., Seyfang, G., & Smith, A. (2012). Exploring the Roles of Intermediaries in UK Community Energy: Grassroots Innovations and Niche Development. *Science, Society & Sustainability, 23*, 1–26.

Hekkert, M. P., Suurs, R. A. A., Negro, S. O., Kuhlmann, S., & Smits, R. E. H. M. (2007). Functions of Innovation Systems: A New Approach for Analysing Technological Change. *Technological Forecasting and Social Change, 74*, 413–432. https://doi.org/10.1016/j.techfore.2006.03.002.

Hossain, M. (2017). Technological Forecasting & Social Change Motivations, Challenges, and Opportunities of Successful Solvers on an Innovation Intermediary Platform. *Technological Forecasting and Social Change*. https://doi.org/10.1109/ICEOE.2011.6013395.

Howells, J. (2006). Intermediation and the Role of Intermediaries in Innovation. *Research Policy, 35*, 715–728. https://doi.org/10.1016/j.respol.2006.03.005.

Iturrioz, C., Aragón, C., & Narvaiza, L. (2015). How to Foster Shared Innovation Within SMEs' Networks: Social Capital and the Role of Intermediaries. *European Management Journal, 33*, 104–115. https://doi.org/10.1016/j.emj.2014.09.003.

Katzy, B., Turgut, E., Holzmann, T., & Sailer, K. (2013). Innovation Intermediaries: A Process View on Open Innovation Coordination. *Technology Analysis & Strategic Management, 25*, 295–309. https://doi.org/10.1080/09537325.2013.764982.

Kerry, C., & Danson, M. (2016). Open Innovation, Triple Helix and Regional Innovation Systems. *Industry and Higher Education, 30*, 67–78. https://doi.org/10.5367/ihe.2016.0292.

Kilelu, C. W., Klerkx, L., Leeuwis, C., & Hall, A. (2011). Beyond Knowledge Brokering: An Exploratory Study on Innovation Intermediaries in an Evolving Smallholder Agricultural System in Kenya. *Knowledge Management for Development Journal, 7*, 84–108. https://doi.org/10.1080/19474199.2011.593859.

Kim, E. S. (2015). *Facilitating Innovation in SMEs: The Case of Public Intermediaries in South Korea* [Doctoral Thesis]. Edinburgh: The University of Edinburgh.

Kivimaa, P. (2014). Government-Affiliated Intermediary Organisations as Actors in System-Level Transitions. *Research Policy, 43*, 1370–1380. https://doi.org/10.1016/j.respol.2014.02.007.

Klerkx, L., Álvarez, R., & Campusano, R. (2015). The Emergence and Functioning of Innovation Intermediaries in Maturing Innovation Systems: The Case of Chile. *Innovation and Development, 5*, 73–91. https://doi.org/10.1080/2157930X.2014.921268.

Klewitz, J., Zeyen, A., & Hansen, E. G. (2013). Intermediaries Driving Eco-Innovation in SMEs: A Qualitative Investigation. *European Journal of Innovation Management, 15*, 442–467. https://doi.org/10.1108/14601061211272376.

Kokshagina, O., & Le Masson, P. (2015). Fast-Connecting Open Innovation Practices: On the Role of Intermediaries to Accelerate the Absorptive Capacity Function. *ISPIM Conference, 120*, 232–239.

Lee, S., Park, G., Yoon, B., & Park, J. (2010). Open Innovation in SMEs-an Intermediated Network Model. *Research Policy, 39*, 290–300. https://doi.org/10.1016/j.respol.2009.12.009.

Lin, H., Zeng, S., Liu, H., & Li, C. (2016). How Do Intermediaries Drive Corporate Innovation? A Moderated Mediating Examination. *Journal of Business Research, 69*, 4831–4836. https://doi.org/10.1016/j.jbusres.2016.04.039.

Love, J. H., & Roper, S. (2015). SME Innovation, Exporting and Growth: A Review of Existing Evidence. *International Small Business Journal, 33*, 28–48. https://doi.org/10.1177/0266242614550190.

Lukkarinen, J., Berg, A., Salo, M., Tainio, P., Alhola, K., & Antikainen, R. (2018). An Intermediary Approach to Technological Innovation Systems (TIS)—The Case of the Cleantech Sector in Finland. In *Environmental Innovation and Societal Transitions* (pp. 136–146). https://doi.org/10.1016/j.eist.2017.04.003.

Lundvall, B. Å., Johnson, B., Andersen, E. S., & Dalum, B. (2002). National Systems of Production, Innovation and Competence Building. *Research Policy, 31*, 213–231. https://doi.org/10.1016/S0048-7333(01)00137-8.

Malerba, F. (2002). Sectoral Systems of Innovation and Production. *Research Policy, 31*, 247–264.

Malerba, F. (2004). *Sectoral Systems of Innovation: Concepts, Issues and Analyses of Six Major Sectors in Europe*. Cambridge: Cambridge University Press. https://doi.org/10.1017/CBO9780511493270.

Malerba, F. (2005). Sectoral Systems of Innovation: A Framework for Linking Innovation to the Knowledge Base, Structure and Dynamics of Sectors. *Economics of Innovation and New Technology, 14*, 63–82. https://doi.org/10.1080/1043859042000228688.

Malerba, F., & McKelvey, M. (2020). Knowledge-Intensive Innovative Entrepreneurship Integrating Schumpeter, Evolutionary Economics, and Innovation Systems. *Small Business Economics, 54*, 503–522. https://doi.org/10.1007/s11187-018-0060-2.

Malerba, F., & Orsenigo, L. (1995). Schumpeterian Patterns of Innovation. *Cambridge Journal of Economics, 19*, 47–65. https://doi.org/10.1093/oxfordjournals.cje.a035308.

Malerba, F., Caloghirou, Y., McKelvey, M., & Radoševic, S. (2015). *Dynamics of Knowledge Intensive Entrepreneurship: Business Strategy and Public Policy*. London: Routledge.

Martin, S., & Scott, J. T. J. T. (2000). The Nature of Innovation Market Failure and the Design of Public Support for Private Innovation. *Research Policy, 29*, 437–447. https://doi.org/10.1016/S0048-7333(99)00084-0.

Mazzucato, M., & Penna, C. C. R. (2016). Beyond Market Failures: The Market Creating and Shaping Roles of State Investment Banks. *Journal of Economic Policy Reform, 19*, 305–326. https://doi.org/10.1080/17487870.2016.1216416.

Mgumia, A. H., Mattee, A. Z., & Kundi, B. A. T. (2015). Contribution of Innovation Intermediaries in Agricultural Innovation: The Case of Agricultural R&D in Tanzania. *African Journal of Science, Technology, Innovation and Development, 7*, 151–160. https://doi.org/10.1080/20421338.2015.1023644.

Neffke, F., Hartog, M., Boschma, R., & Henning, M. (2014). *The Role of Firms and Entrepreneurs in Regional Diversification*. Utrecht: Utrecht University, Section of Economic Geography.

Nelson, R. R. (1993). *National Innovation Systems: A Comparative Analysis*. University of Illinois at Urbana-Champaign's Academy for Entrepreneurial Leadership Historical Research Reference in Entrepreneurship. Champaign, IL: University of Illinois.

Ngwenya, H., & Hagmann, J. (2011). Making Innovation Systems Work in Practice: Experiences in Integrating Innovation, Social Learning and Knowledge in Innovation Platforms. *Knowledge Management for Development Journal, 7*, 109–124. https://doi.org/10.1080/19474199.2011.593867.

Nilsson, M., & Sia-Ljungström, C. (2013, February 18–23). The Role of Innovation Intermediaries in Innovation Systems. In *2013 International European Forum* (pp. 161–180). Innsbruck/Igls: International European Forum on System Dynamics and Innovation in Food Networks.

Pavitt, K. (2003). *The Process of Innovation*. SPRU Working Paper Series, SPRU—Science Policy Research Unit, University of Sussex Business School.

Radosevic, S. (2017). Assessing EU Smart Specialisation Policy in a Comparative Perspective. In S. Radosevic, A. Curaj, L. Andreescu, & R. Gheorgiu (Eds.), *Advances in the Theory and Practice of Smart Specialization*. London: Elsevier.

Smits, R., & Kuhlmann, S. (2004). The Rise of Systemic Instruments in Innovation Policy. *International Journal of Foresight and Innovation Policy, 1*, 4. https://doi.org/10.1504/IJFIP.2004.004621.

Stojčić, N., & Aralica, Z. (2018). (De)Industrialisation and Lessons for Industrial Policy in Central and Eastern Europe. *Post-Communist Economies, 30*, 713–734. https://doi.org/10.1080/14631377.2018.1443251.

Swann, G. M. P. (2009). *The Economics of Innovation: An Introduction, 2009.* New York: Edward Elgar Publishing. https://doi.org/10.1556/AOecon.60.2010.4.6.

Thérin, F. (2007). *Handbook of Research on Techno-Entrepreneurship*. New York: Elgar Edward Publishing.

Tsujimoto, M., Kajikawa, Y., Tomita, J., & Matsumoto, Y. (2018). A Review of the Ecosystem Concept—Towards Coherent Ecosystem Design. *Technological Forecasting and Social Change, 136*, 49–58. https://doi.org/10.1016/j.techfore.2017.06.032.

Tullock, G., Brady, G., & Seldon, A. (2002). Government Failure: A Primer in Public Choice. Washington, D.C.: Cato Institute

Van der Meulen, B., Nedeva, M., Braun, D., van der Meulen, B., Nedeva, M., & Braun, D. (2005). *Intermediaries Organisation and Processes: Theory and Research Issues*. PRIME Workshop.

Venturini, K., & Verbano, C. (2014). A Systematic Review of the Space Technology Transfer Literature: Research Synthesis and Emerging Gaps. *Space Policy, 30*, 98–114. https://doi.org/10.1016/j.spacepol.2014.04.003.

Vidmar, M. (2019). Agile Space Living Lab—The Emergence of a New High-Tech Innovation Paradigm. *Space Policy, 49*, 101324

Vidmar, M. (2020). New Space and Innovation Policy: Scotland's Emerging "Space Glen". *New Space, 8*, 31–51. https://doi.org/10.1089/space.2019.0032.

Vidmar, M., Rosiello, A., Williams, R., Vermeulen, N., & Dines, J. (2020). New Space and Agile Innovation: Understanding Transition to Open Innovation Through Examining Innovation Networks and Moments. *Acta Astronautica, 167*, 122–134.

West, J., Salter, A., Vanhaverbek, W., & Chesbrough, H. (2014). Open Innovation: The Next Decade. *Research Policy, 43*, 805–811. https://doi.org/10.1016/J.RESPOL.2014.03.001.

Wright, M., Roper, S., Hart, M., & Carter, S. (2015). Joining the Dots: Building the Evidence Base for SME Growth Policy. *International Small Business Journal, 33*, 3–11. https://doi.org/10.1177/0266242614558316.

CHAPTER 2

What Are Innovation Intermediaries?

Abstract This chapter provides an overview of the evolving definition of what is an innovation intermediary and proposes its further extension to address the challenges of fragmentation of roles and activities of these organisations. In particular, it extends the core definition of innovation intermediation to cover activities beyond the multi-party (knowledge) brokerage. Subsequently, it analyses past systematisation of innovation intermediaries and their activities, finding them lacking in comprehensiveness and clarity. Finally, it proposes to shift the focus of analysis from roles and functions and towards innovation intermediaries interventions.

Keywords Definition of innovation intermediation • Innovation moments • Systematisation of innovation intermediaries • Intermediation interventions

Academics studying the processes of innovation have for decades been examining the activities and roles of innovation intermediaries. These are an eclectic group of organisations involved in the development of new products and their marketisation, who are neither the instigators nor the beneficiaries of the innovation itself. Instead, they intermediate between the various participants and try to smooth and accelerate the development of products and services, companies and sectors. Innovation

M. Vidmar, *Innovation Intermediaries and (Final) Frontiers of High-tech*, https://doi.org/10.1007/978-3-030-60642-8_2

intermediaries can be defined in many different ways. The seminal definition was proposed in the influential paper "Intermediation and the Role of Intermediaries in Innovation" by Howells (2006). His premise is that an innovation intermediary is:

> *An organization or body that acts as an agent or broker in any aspect of the innovation process between two or more parties.* (Howells 2006, p. 720)

Howells bases this definition on a very large review of past studies, which suggests that intermediaries' primary roles are multi-party (knowledge) brokerage (Howells 2006). This rationale is further underpinned by the observation that key processes of open innovation (Chesbrough 2011; Chesbrough and Bogers 2014; Helfat and Quinn 2006), in particular at Small and Medium Enterprises (SMEs) level (Lee et al. 2010), are based on interaction with external partners (West and Bogers 2014). Knowledge dissipation from research activities, in particular, is done through such interlinking between individuals and organisations (Brown and Duguid 2001; Malerba 2005). Hence Open Innovation is crucially linked to the network of external partners from whom a company can source knowledge and/or with whom it can share its own resources (Iturrioz et al. 2015; Tidd et al. 2005). This is a key element of the innovation systems view of Open Innovation, of which a key component is the knowledge network and its density or interconnectedness (Inkpen and Tsang 2005; Kim 2015; Pittaway et al. 2004; Simard and West 2006).

Starting from the prevailing knowledge brokerage conceptualisation, this chapter first analyses the significance of knowledge in the innovation process, before moving beyond its exclusive focus in innovation intermediation studies. In fact, by expanding the definition of innovation intermediary a plethora of other activities and systemic roles also covered by innovation intermediaries are explored. Furthermore, past attempts at systematising intermediaries are analysed, exposing a lack of comprehensiveness, clarity and contextualisation. Hence, it is proposed that the attention shifts to innovation intermediaries' interventions (rather than their roles or functions) as the grounding analytical conceptualisation.

Innovation Moments, Organisational Learning and Knowledge Brokerage

As high-tech SMEs are more dependent on external support in innovation processes, these processes can be best understood using a contextual/network study approach which examines their interaction with other actors (Lee et al. 2010; Pullen et al. 2012; van de Vrande et al. 2009). In particular, to bring together insights from different strands of organisational learning and knowledge and technology management in capturing the structure of an interconnected innovation process, the innovation moments framework has been proposed (Vidmar et al. 2020).

Innovation Moments and New Product Development in SMEs

In the classic innovation literature, the processes of organisational learning and knowledge management within new product development (NPD) processes were framed in a linear or cyclical fashion, though neither framing alone was accepted as a sufficiently full account (Pavitt 2006). Instead, empirical studies have found that fuzzy/messy and complex dynamical processes govern NPD in SMEs (Swann 2009). The linear-cyclical dichotomy can be deconstructed into a new phased/modular approach, with linearly overlapping stages and cyclically repeating work processes, which combines the schematic clarity of past models with capturing more of the fuzziness/messiness—this is the gist of the innovation moments approach.

This emerging framing is also related to the state of the art in knowledge management literature, for instance, Nonaka's (Nonaka et al. 1998) typology with socialisation, externalisation, combination and internalisation of knowledge as the key elements. It also incorporates Sun and Anderson's (Sun and Anderson 2010) merger of lead organisational learning theories with the absorptive capacity framework, that is the ability of firms to source and integrate new knowledge from the external environment. Specifically, Sun and Anderson align the organisational learning processes of intuiting, interpreting, integrating and institutionalising knowledge from Crossan et al. (Crossan et al. 1999) with Zahra and George's understanding of absorptive capacity through acquisition, assimilation, transformation and exploitation of knowledge (Zahra and George 2002).

(*continued*)

(continued)

The proposed conceptualisation is based on a sequence of innovation moments (Edwards 2000; Edwards et al. 2005) developing a linear trajectory of NPD. These can be formalised phases of NPD processes—such as defining users' technical requirements, building a prototype, beta testing—or a series of problem-solving activities addressing technical/R&D or commercial/business development challenges for the progression of an NPD project. The cyclicity can be seen in the framing of the four key elements of each innovation moment as a developmental build-up from problem definition, following through expertise gathering and solution formation towards integration in the next phase of the process (as seen in the schema below). By structuring NPD as a linear progression of problem-solving exercises, innovation moment framework can be used to relate knowledge and technology absorption and management processes to the wider NPD process.

Innovation Moment's Internal Cycle

1. ***Defining*** *the problem/idea (identification)*
2. ***Gathering*** *the required expertise (acquisition)*
3. ***Forming*** *applicable solutions (selection)*
4. ***Integrating*** *into the developed product (alignment)*

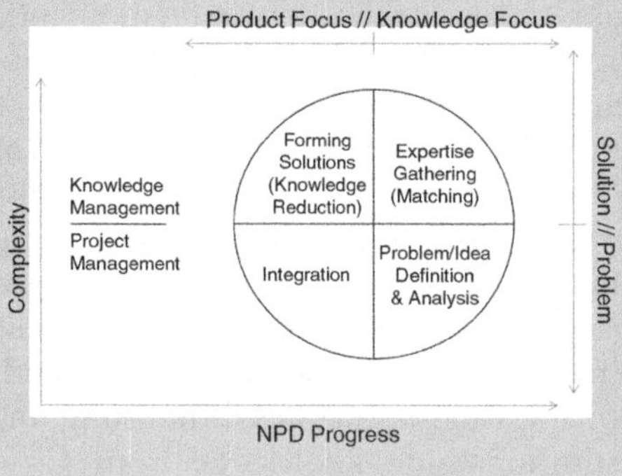

Though openness has been a critical interest in the development of science and advancement in technology, more detailed understanding of the mechanics of the cultural changes it relates to has been primarely rooted in the context of large-scale corporations of the industrial and post-industrial era (Hossain and Kauranen 2016; Parida et al. 2012). In contrast, the current economic system relies significantly on bottom-up innovation from SMEs, working in a closely linked innovation (eco)system with academic research organisations, regulators and government, and lead customers and users. This model has been described as the triple helix (Leydesdorff and Etzkowitz 1995) and has recently become a leading interest within research in support for Open Innovation, in particular through the interconnecting role of innovation intermediaries (Kerry and Danson 2016).

Building on the importance of knowledge brokerage, an SME's ability to share and absorb knowledge from an open innovation network is seen as a precondition for regional industrial development (Von Tunzelmann 2009). It follows that pathways through which the knowledge is brought into an innovation network or transferred across sectoral and technological domains also play a key role in the SMEs' innovation and NPD processes. Past studies highlight that new combinations of knowledge tend to happen at the interfaces of both geographically proximate and cognitively related domains (Boschma and Frenken 2011; Cooke 2012). To bridge these domains SMEs often need translational support, which intermediaries are providing in their knowledge brokering function (Howells 2006; Kim 2015).

Whilst the criticality of knowledge and technology brokerage in an ecosystem is not to be underestimated, substantive literature already exists to examine it in more detail. For instance, Bekkers and Bodas Freitas (2008) identify some twenty-three distinct channels for knowledge and technology transfer, giving rise to at least as many types of intermediaries actions. However, due to the extent of academic interest in knowledge creation, dissemination and utilisation/exploitation the innovation intermediation is often reduced to facilitating such. In contrast, as explored in the next section, looking beyond the knowledge brokerage allows us to develop a more comprehensive picture of innovation intermediation activities.

Innovation Intermediation Beyond Knowledge Brokerage

A series of studies have shown that intermediaries engage with their sectors far beyond the knowledge brokerage definition described above and that many interventions take on a wider systemic role (Dosi et al. 2006; Smits and Kuhlmann 2004). In particular, there is a significant amount of work demonstrating not only the breadth, but also the depth of intermediaries' involvement in knowledge production (Agogué et al. 2013; Deschamps et al. 2013; Hyysalo and Stewart 2008) and their hands-on support and management of collaborations and projects (Katzy et al. 2013; Mgumia et al. 2015).

Furthermore, there is a plethora of research examining many other ways through which intermediaries support SMEs and their innovation processes. Crucial examples focus on support with "locating and approaching the customer, developing relationships of trust, accessing finance, effectively managing the firm, and training employees" (Vonortas 2002); provision of specialist equipment (Mian 1996); quality control, standards development and certification (Fuchs 2009; Grindley et al. 1994; McEvily and Zaheer 1999); providing physical space (Löfsten and Lindelöf 2002); as well as engaging in sectoral brand development and developing regulatory (legal) frameworks (Boon et al. 2011; Lukkarinen et al. 2018; Sapsed et al. 2007).

The deployment of these resources and activities, whilst related to development and maintenance of a knowledge-based innovation network, is much more diverse than the brokerage function. Howells makes the distinction that knowledge-brokerage-based innovation intermediation can be one of the functions of organisations providing wider innovation support (Howells 2006). However, it is becoming clear from the studies listed in the previous paragraph that these additional activities are an intrinsic part of systemic intermediation itself. Hence, it is proposed that a more inclusive definition is more appropriate in developing a holistic understanding of the variety and complexity of intermediaries' work. This is in line with Dalziel, who states that:

> *Innovation intermediaries are organizations or groups within organizations that work to enable innovation, either directly by enabling the innovativeness of one or more firms, or indirectly by enhancing the innovative capacity of regions, nations, or sectors.* (Dalziel 2010, p. 1)

This broader definition is also allowing for a variety of programmes enabling business development and market creation to be included. Dalziel, for instance, mentions industry and trade associations, economic development agencies, chambers of commerce, science (or technology or business) parks, business incubators, research consortia and networks, research institutes and standards organisations (Dalziel 2010). This indicates that the definition could be expanded based on the multiple and varied functions identified in the literature review and the academic and practitioners' interest to comprehensively address the variety of functional roles innovation intermediaries undertake within innovation systems. Hence, the definition should be further amended to state that:

> *An innovation intermediary is an organisation or a group within an organisation, whose main objective is to carry out interventions enabling innovation, either directly by enabling the innovativeness of one or more firms, or indirectly by enhancing the innovative capacity of regions, nations, or sectors.*

This expanded definition crucially introduces a key new analytical marker namely the main purpose or objective, which is also corresponding to Howells' (2006) notion of central and peripheral functions within many organisations in this arena and echoing Winch and Courtney's definition, highlighting that innovation intermediaries are "focused neither on the generation nor the implementation of innovations, but on enabling other organizations to innovate" (Winch and Courtney 2007, p. 751). In addition, the proposed new definition also specifies more clearly that an intermediary's work is to intervene in the system, with the variety of interventions aimed to enable innovation—including those moving away from brokerage—becoming the key objects of innovation intermediation research.

Making Sense of Innovation Intermediaries and Their Activities

Many attempts have been made so far by different authors to classify the various intermediaries' interventions into organised groups, related by activity, intent/objectives or other parameters (Dalziel 2010; Howells 2006; Kilelu et al. 2011; Kim 2015; Kivimaa 2014; Lukkarinen et al. 2018; Nilsson and Sia-Ljungström 2013). For example, when looking at innovation intermediaries interventions, Dalziel identifies three key areas of activity for intermediaries (Dalziel 2010):

- Inter-organisational networking activities
- Technology development (and related activities)
- Other activities[1]

[1] This last category is labelled here as "Business Development Provision", as the interventions listed in this group are mainly concerning the running of the business operation and

However, this classification seems incomplete in the range of interventions included as well as overly simplistic in terms of categorisation. While their analysis is helpful in terms of providing a concrete programmatic analysis of what intermediaries can do to support innovation, their focus on networking is detracting from other modes of engagement intermediaries' undertake, in particular in wider socio-political engagement.

In a more complete manner, Howells (2006) lists the following "typology of intermediation in innovation process":

- Foresight and diagnosis
- Scanning and information processing
- Knowledge processing, generation and combination
- Gatekeeping and brokering
- Testing, validation and training
- Accreditation and standards
- Regulation and arbitration
- Intellectual property: protecting the results
- Commercialisation: exploiting the outcomes
- Assessment and evaluation

Conversely, the above list is less of a classification and more of a list of functions, and even as such its complexity does not positively contribute to the deficit of theoretical and operational clarity described earlier. Hence, starting from Howells (2006) and expanding on it, Lopez-Vega identified three categories of intermediaries functions (Lopez-Vega 2009):

- Functions which facilitate the collaboration between organisations
- Functions which involve connecting services between an organisation and its environment
- Functions which provide various services to stakeholders

However, the extensive focus on knowledge brokerage and social learning further limits this analysis to social activities and soft capital (i.e. knowledge, information, know-how, status, contacts, etc.). Dalziel's analysis, for instance, also includes the provision of physical space and equipment as a very significant type of intervention (Dalziel 2010). In a similar manner Kilelu et al. conclude that:

human resources development. See Annex 1 for full classification.

Following a comprehensive review of various authors who have looked at roles and functions of intermediaries and brokers in supporting and managing innovation processes (van Lente et al. 2003*; Smits and Kuhlmann* 2004*; Howells* 2006*; Klerkx and Leeuwis* 2008*; Kristjanson et al.* 2009*), we noted six broad functions, namely:*

- *Demand articulation/stimulation*
- *Network brokering*
- *Knowledge brokering*
- *Innovation process management*
- *Capacity building*
- *Institutional building* (Kilelu et al. 2011, p. 13)

Kilelu et al.'s classification is far more promising than the ones suggested earlier, as the systemic functions listed here are clearly linked to a proposed four-dimensional intermediaries' typology (Kilelu et al. 2011), with Systemic Brokers, Technology Brokers, Enterprise Development Support and Input Access-Focused Intermediaries identified as the four distinct types.[2] However, the issue with these two approaches is that they link interventions' functions with organisational dynamics, instead of producing a typology of interventions themselves, which can be deployed independently of each other responding to a wider systemic dynamics and simultaneously perform different roles and functions.

Furthermore, as these attempts often start with Howells' (2006) classification, the analyses frequently do not include some of the available interventions, in particular, provision of physical space and equipment. This latter issue can be found in Kivimaa typology as well, though it otherwise does helpfully link functions with four groups/classes of interventions—that is, Articulation of expectations and visions, Building of social networks, Learning processes and exploration at multiple dimensions and Other (Kivimaa 2014). However, also noted is that this typology is also cumbersome to implement, as its systematisation does not propose any

[2] There is a similar typology derived empirically by Colombo et al. (2015), who define four intermediary types as Connector (gather information regarding the experience and competences), Broker (identify the sources of knowledge), Collector (provide solutions) and Mediator (establish a relationship). Another such typology is forwarded by Kim (2015) who describes four overarching "roles" as: Knowledge enabling, Facilitating relations, Facilitating learning, Managing interfaces.

substantive sub-divisions of interventions, leaving a plethora of examples from past studies un-harmonised.

There is also a new strand of Open Innovation literature centred on living laboratory conceptualisation of innovation process (Bergvall-Kåreborn et al. 2009; Dell'Era and Landoni 2014; Eriksson et al. 2006; Vidmar 2019)—including a wider variety of stakeholders and extending the innovation process beyond the design stage into the field of use, sometimes referred to as innofusion (Fleck 1993). Starting from the Howells' (2006) seminal work, authors in this field also note that organisations facilitating such laboratories act as innovation intermediaries (Hyysalo and Stewart 2008). Building on a previous systematisation by Heikkinen et al. (2007), Nyström et al. (2014) developed a classification with 17 different roles:

1. *Webber: Acts as the initiator; decides on potential actors*
2. *Instigator: Influences actors' decision-making processes*
3. *Gatekeeper: Possesses resources*
4. *Advocate: Background role; distributes information externally*
5. *Producer: Contributes to the development process*
6. *Planner: Participates in development processes; input in the form of intangible resources*
7. *Accessory provider: Self-motivated to promote its products, services, and expertise*
8. *Coordinator: Coordinates a group of participants*
9. *Builder: Establishes and promotes the emergence of close relationships between various participants in the living lab*
10. *Messenger: Forwards and disseminates information in the living lab network*
11. *Facilitator: Offers resources for the use of the network*
12. *Orchestrator: Guides and supports the network's activities and continuation; tries to establish trust in the network to boost collaboration to further the living lab's goals*
13. *Integrator: Integrates heterogeneous knowledge, development ideas, technologies, or outputs of different living lab actors into a functional entity*
14. *Informant: Brings users' knowledge, understanding, and opinions to the living lab*
15. *Tester: Tests innovation in (customers') real-life environments (e.g., hospitals, student restaurants, and classrooms)*

16. *Contributor: Collaborates intensively with the other actors in the network to develop new products, services, processes, or technologies*
17. *Co-creator: The user co-designs a service, product, or process together with the company's R&D team and the other living lab actors.* (Hakkarainen and Hyysalo 2016)

Hakkarainen and Hyysalo (2016) empirically identify no fewer than "13 different intermediary activities and 31 tasks" loosely based on the above classification. They highlight the now familiar critical observation across this field that:

> *the granularity of the findings has remained coarse and has resulted in "naming theory" of identifying lists of "actor roles". Following Gregor's (2002) framework for theory development, this is the most rudimentary form of theory in a given area that merely answers "what" questions.* (Hakkarainen and Hyysalo 2016, p. 56)

Though taking this criticism on board Hakkarainen and Hyysalo (2016) do develop a set of detailed analysis as to "how" innovation intermediaries operate within the context of a living lab and the evolution of their activities, however, critical "what" questions, such as what are the common factors amongst the different activities and "what" are particular outcomes remain unanswered.

Deploying a different approach, starting from the innovation systems features and attempting to fit intermediaries' activities to them, Nilsson and Sia-Ljungström (2013) highlight that:

> *Bergek et al. and Hekkert et al. provide inventories of system functions, including: Knowledge development and diffusion; Entrepreneurial experimentation; System infrastructure creation; Influence on the direction of search; Market formation; Legitimation; Resource mobilization; and Development of positive externalities/synergies.* (Nilsson and Sia-Ljungström 2013, p. 163)

Their subsequent analysis of intermediaries' operations based on these pre-identified system functions provides a more board insight into the variety of available interventions, though they note the slight disconnect between the operational activities the intermediaries deploy and the more abstract system features. They specifically comment on

> *the need for further work on understanding not only to the extent these innovation system functions are fulfilled by innovation intermediaries but also the magnitude, the type of interaction and the indirect effects these activities can have on the innovation system.* (Nilsson and Sia-Ljungström 2013, pp. 171–172)

Hence, the approach here to developing further understanding of innovation intermediation marks a clear attempt to transcend the three identified issues:

- The incompleteness of analysed array of interventions
- Lack of clarity in classification
- Lack of links between available interventions and their systemic functions

The key analytical tool needed for developing an improved advanced systematisation is a functional classification system, expanding on the ones presented above, which would encompass all available interventions, yet retain theoretical and operational clarity. In order to embed such clarity of function in the classification, the latter has to be linked to a true framework of the established classes of interventions, which takes into consideration practitioners' concerns and their policy requirements as well as operational constraints (Klewitz et al. 2013). These may relate to scale and intensity of engagement within a given intervention, the two being in approximate inverse correlation, or ability to deploy particular types of resources and activities.[3]

From Roles to Interventions

To summarise the analysis in the previous sections, there are many different types of intermediaries' functions, and in most cases, their work spans several categories of resources provision and active participation in an innovation system. Furthermore, intermediaries' roles change due to a myriad of external and internal factors and evolve as an innovation system is developing. Arguably, their role is most crucial in the early, that is emergent, stage of an innovation system (Agogué et al. 2013; Antikaninen

[3] A more complete classification and typology emerging from this framework will be presented in Chap. 4.

et al. 2009; Katzy et al. 2013), but there are many roles they can and do fulfil in mature systems as well (Boon et al. 2011; Vonortas 2002).

To move beyond the challenges of sorting out institutional roles and configurations, it may be more pertinent and central to the understanding of the innovation intermediaries to focus on their interventions in the innovation system, rather than study their organisational structure. This somewhat functionalist take on the literature is further inspired by a growing need for clarity amongst the practitioner stakeholders, whose diverse organisational backgrounds nonetheless converge in the questions of what should we do to achieve a certain result in a given context (Agogué et al. 2017; Dalziel 2010; Hargreaves et al. 2012; Klewitz et al. 2013)? Furthermore, the scattered literature across this field is exposing another struggle—to consistently define the role(s) intermediaries play in these systems. These roles and functions are well established when it comes to the knowledge brokerage model, but they break down when a broader systemic view is taken. This leaves a significant amount of studies unaccounted for in innovation intermediaries' literature reviews and hence, out of touch with the theoretical—and consequently also operational—developments.

Hence, this book is centered on a proposition to ground the analysis of intermediation on the conceptualisation of an intervention, which is defined as any activity intended to bring about a change in the operation of a social system. This very broad definition has origins in public policy literature, though has been used in the innovation domain as well (Chaminade and Esquist 2006; Hanley et al. 2015; Mgumia et al. 2015; Wang 2018). Crucially, it encompasses many different types of interventions from broader framework development, such as economic incentives or legal changes, to direct activities carried out with multiple parties or participants.

Interventions are (or at least should be) underpinned by a clear theory of change (Brousselle and Champagne 2011; Clark and Taplin 2012; Jackson 2013). Theories of change provide justification for interventions and use logic modelling or other tools to map the proposed action against expected outcomes—a cornerstone of innovation policy (Autio et al. 2008; Edler et al. 2013; Russo and Rossi 2009). It is important to note that any realistic interventions can rarely be the sole cause of a particular outcome, rather they contribute to it, as can be examined by contribution analysis (Brousselle and Champagne 2011). Hence, a theory of change is premised on the causal attribution reasoning, which defines a contribution of the intervention towards the desired effect: good theories of change have clearly identified (pre-)conditions, rationales for available intervention(s) and measurable indicators linked to specific outcomes or impacts (Clark and Taplin 2012). Each particular intervention requires a bespoke instance of a theory of change proposition, responding to the existing circumstances within which the intervention will be deployed, though the theory's elements, i.e. available tools to achieve a certain goal, can be adopted from a generic pool.

This broader framing successfully includes all deployments of activities and resources put forward by innovation intermediaries. The reasoning or theory of change behind their interventions is the intention to change the innovation landscape on macro, meso or micro level, as well as deliver specific economic, political and social outcomes. On the one hand, such mandate for, and investment in, change is based on the available financial and social capital. On the other hand, the intervention's objectives depend on the analysis of the existing context or environment and the available theoretical and empirical understanding of possible and available interventions, though this often includes political/ideological considerations and not merely evidence (Howells 2006).

Hence, a successful intervention-setting requires an in-depth analysis of the contextual environment followed by a transparent decision making on the appropriateness of a specific intervention given the available understanding. However, the latter is sorely lacking, in particular, as noted by Hannon, Skea and Rhodes (2014) referring to further evidence from several studies:

> *"the literature is currently too fragmented (Howells* 2006*; Van der Meulen et al.* 2005*) [...]" and "we possess only a limited 'understanding of these entities, their role, their functions, and their activities in different contexts'".* (Abbate et al. 2013, p. 235; Hannon et al. 2014, p. 8)

In particular, as dynamic and pro-active organisations, innovation intermediaries are often closely aligned to other aspects of public life, especially politics and economy, and their stability and endurance in a great part depend on their ability to adapt and morph with time (Howells 2006). This is underpinned by processes of social learning (Hyysalo and Stewart 2008; Ngwenya and Hagmann 2011). Hence, an evidence-based systematisation of the intermediaries' interventions is needed in order to enable both the advancement of our theoretical and empirical understanding of intermediaries and their interventions as well as assisting in the operational deployment of the current literature.

In summary, innovation intermediaries should be thought of as in the broadest set of organisational groups which engage in innovation processes, without being either originators or benefactors of them. However, as seen from the analysis of past definitions, the function or role-driven understanding of these organisations makes understanding their structure and activities challenging. In the next chapter, the existing state of the art will be deployed to try to make sense of a case study of New Space sector in Scotland, to illustrate what innovation intermediaries look like in practice, as well as point to the critical questions of their understanding within the context of Geographically-Bound Sectoral Systems of Innovation.

Bibliography

Abbate, T., Coppolino, R., & Schiavone, F. (2013). Linking Entities in Knowledge Transfer: The Innovation Intermediaries. *Journal of the Knowledge Economy, 4*, 233–243. https://doi.org/10.1007/s13132-013-0156-5.

Agogué, M., Ystrom, A., & Le Masson, P. (2013). Rethinking the Role of Intermediaries as an Architect of Collective Exploration and Creation of Knowledge in Open Innovation. *International Journal of Innovation Management, 17*, 1350007. https://doi.org/10.1142/S1363919613500072.

Agogué, M., Berthet, E., Fredberg, T., Le Masson, P., Segrestin, B., Stoetzel, M., Wiener, M., & Yström, A. (2017). Explicating the Role of Innovation Intermediaries in the "Unknown": A Contingency Approach. *Journal of Strategy and Management, 10*, 19–39. https://doi.org/10.1108/JSMA-01-2015-0005.

Antikaninen, M., Mäkipää, M., & Ahonen, M. (2009). Motivating and Supporting Collaboration in Open Innovation. *Technology Management, 13*, 24.

Autio, E., Kanninen, S., & Gustafsson, R. (2008). First- and Second-Order Additionality and Learning Outcomes in Collaborative RD Programs. *Research Policy, 37*, 59–76. https://doi.org/10.1016/J.RESPOL.2007.07.012.

Bekkers, R., & Bodas Freitas, I. M. (2008). Analysing Knowledge Transfer Channels Between Universities and Industry: To What Degree Do Sectors Also Matter? *Research Policy, 37*, 1837–1853. https://doi.org/10.1016/j.respol.2008.07.007.

Bergvall-Kåreborn, B., Ihlström Eriksson, C., Ståhlbröst, A., & Lund, J. (2009). A Milieu for Innovation—Defining Living Labs. In *2nd ISPIM Innovation Symposium* (pp. 6–9). New York.

Boon, W. P., Moors, E. H., Kuhlmann, S., & Smits, R. E. (2011). Demand Articulation in Emerging Technologies: Intermediary User Organisations as Co-Producers? *Research Policy, 40*, 242–252.

Boschma, R., & Frenken, K. (2011). Technological Relatedness, Related Variety and Economic Geography. In P. Cooke, B. T. Asheim, R. Boschma, R. Martin, D. Schwartz, & F. Tdtling (Eds.), *Handbook of Regional Innovation and Growth* (pp. 187–197). London: Edward Elgar Publishing. https://doi.org/10.1093/jeg/lbq053.

Brousselle, A., & Champagne, F. (2011). Program Theory Evaluation: Logic Analysis. *Evaluation and Program Planning, 34*, 69–78. https://doi.org/10.1016/j.evalprogplan.2010.04.001.

Brown, J. S., & Duguid, P. (2001). Knowledge and Organization: A Social-Practice Perspective. *Organization Science, 12*, 198–213. https://doi.org/10.1287/orsc.12.2.198.10116.

Chaminade, C., & Esquist, C. (2006). *Rationales for Public Policy Intervention in the Innovation Process: Systems of Innovation Approach, the Theory and Practice of Innovation Policy*. CIRCLE, Lund University. https://doi.org/10.4337/9781849804424.00012.

Chesbrough, H. (2011). Everything You Need to Know About Open Innovation. Forbes.com

Chesbrough, H., & Bogers, M. (2014). *Explicating Open Innovation: Clarifying an Emerging Paradigm for Understanding Innovation, New Frontiers in Open Innovation*. Oxford: Oxford University Press. https://doi.org/10.1093/acprof.

Clark, H., & Taplin, D. (2012). *Theory of Change Basics: A Primer on Theory of Change, ActKnowledge*. New York: Actknowledge. https://doi.org/10.5327/Z201600010002RBM.

Colombo, M. G., Dell'Era, C., & Frattini, F. (2015). Contribution of Innovation Intermediaries to NPD Process. *R&D Management, 45*, 126–146.

Cooke, P. (2012). Knowledge Economy Spillovers, Proximity, and Specialization. In *Interactive Learning for Innovation* (pp. 100–111). London: Palgrave Macmillan. https://doi.org/10.1057/9780230362420_5.

Crossan, M. M., Lane, H. W., & White, R. E. (1999). An Organizational Learning Framework: From Intuition to Institution. *The Academy of Management Review, 24*, 522. https://doi.org/10.2307/259140.

Dalziel, M. (2010). Why Do Innovation Intermediaries Exist? In *Druid 2010: Opening Up Innovation: Strategy, Organization and Technology* (p. 23). London: Imperial College London Business School.

Dell'Era, C., & Landoni, P. (2014). Living Lab: A Methodology Between User-Centred Design and Participatory Design. *Creativity and Innovation Management, 23*, 137–154. https://doi.org/10.1111/caim.12061.

Deschamps, I., Macedo, M. G., & Eve-Levesque, C. (2013). University-SME Collaboration and Open Innovation: Intellectual-Property Management Tools and the Roles of Intermediaries. *Technology Innovation and Management Review, 3*, 33–41.

Dosi, G., Malerba, F., Ramello, G. B., & Silva, F. (2006). Information, Appropriability, and the Generation of Innovative Knowledge Four Decades After Arrow and Nelson: An Introduction. *Industrial and Corporate Change, 15*, 891–901. https://doi.org/10.1093/icc/dtl028.

Edler, J., Cunningham, P., Gök, A., & Shapira, P. (2013). Impacts of Innovation Policy: Synthesis and Conclusions. (Report prepared as part of the project "Compendium of Evidence on the Effectiveness of Innovation Policy Intervention." (NESTA)). Manchester: Manchester Institute of Innovation Research.

Edwards, T. (2000). Innovation and Organizational Change: Developments Towards an Interactive Process Perspective. *Technology Analysis & Strategic Management, 12*, 445–464. https://doi.org/10.1080/713698496.

Edwards, T., Delbridge, R., & Munday, M. (2005). Understanding Innovation in Small and Medium-Sized Enterprise: A Process Manifest. *Technovation, 25*, 1119–1127.

Eriksson, M., Niitamo, V., Kulkki, S., & Hribernik, K. A. (2006). Living Labs as a Multi-Contextual R & D Methodology. In *The 12th International Conference on Concurrent Enterprising: Innovative Products and Services Through Collaborative Networks* (pp. 26–28). ICE. https://doi.org/10.1109/ICE.2006.7477082.

Fleck, J. (1993). Innofusion: Feedback in the Innovation Process. In *Systems Science* (pp. 169–174). Boston: Springer. https://doi.org/10.1007/978-1-4615-2862-3_30.

Fuchs, E. (2009). *The Role of DARPA in Seeding and Encourage New Technology Trajectories.* Sloan Industry Studies Working Papers 2001–2009.

Gregor, S. (2002). A Theory of Theories in Information Systems. In S. Gregor & D. Hart (Eds.), *Information Systems Foundations: Building the Theoretical Base* (pp. 1–20). Canberra, Australia: Australian National University.

Grindley, P., Mowery, D. C., & Silverman, B. (1994). SEMATECH and Collaborative Research: Lessons in the Design of High-Technology Consortia. *Journal of Policy Analysis and Management, 13*, 723. https://doi.org/10.2307/3325495.

Hakkarainen, L., & Hyysalo, S. (2016). The Evolution of Intermediary Activities: Broadening the Concept of Facilitation in Living Labs. *Technology Innovation Management Review, 6*, 45–58.

Hanley, A., Liu, W. H., & Vaona, A. (2015). Credit Depth, Government Intervention and Innovation in China: Evidence from the Provincial Data. *Eurasian Business Review, 5*, 73–98. https://doi.org/10.1007/s40821-015-0016-2.

Hannon, M. J., Skea, J., & Rhodes, A. (2014). Facilitating and Coordinating UK Energy Innovation Through Systemic Innovation Intermediaries. In *International Conference on Sustainability Transitions* (pp. 27–29).

Hargreaves, T., Hielscher, S., Seyfang, G., & Smith, A. (2012). Exploring the Roles of Intermediaries in UK Community Energy: Grassroots Innovations and Niche Development. *Science, Society & Sustainability, 23*, 1–26.

Heikkinen, M. T., Mainela, T., Still, J., & Tähtinen, J. (2007). Roles for Managing in Mobile Service Development Nets. *Industrial Marketing Management, 36*, 909–925. https://doi.org/10.1016/j.indmarman.2007.05.014.

Helfat, C. E., & Quinn, J. B. (2006). *Open Innovation: The New Imperative for Creating and Profiting from TechnologyOpen Innovation: The New Imperative for Creating and Profiting from Technology By Chesbrough Henry*. Boston: Harvard Business School Press, 2003. 227 pages, Hard Cover, $35.00, Academy of Management Perspectives. https://doi.org/10.5465/amp.2006.20591014.

Hossain, M., & Kauranen, I. (2016). Open Innovation in SMEs: A Systematic Literature Review. *Journal of Strategy and Management, 9*, 58–73. https://doi.org/10.1108/JSMA-08-2014-0072.

Howells, J. (2006). Intermediation and the Role of Intermediaries in Innovation. *Research Policy, 35*, 715–728. https://doi.org/10.1016/j.respol.2006.03.005.

Hyysalo, S., & Stewart, J. (2008). Intermediaries, Users and Social Learning in Technological Innovation. *International Journal of Innovation Management, 12*, 295–325. https://doi.org/10.1142/S1363919608002035.

Inkpen, A. C., & Tsang, E. W. K. (2005). Social Capital, Networks, and Knowledge Transfer. *The Academy of Management Review, 30*, 146–165. https://doi.org/10.5465/AMR.2005.15281445.

Iturrioz, C., Aragón, C., & Narvaiza, L. (2015). How to Foster Shared Innovation Within SMEs' Networks: Social Capital and the Role of Intermediaries. *European Management Journal, 33*, 104–115. https://doi.org/10.1016/j.emj.2014.09.003.

Jackson, E. T. (2013). Journal of Sustainable Finance & Interrogating the Theory of Change: Evaluating Impact Investing Where It Matters Most. *Journal of Sustainable Finance & Investment, 3*, 37–41. https://doi.org/10.1080/20430795.2013.776257.

Katzy, B., Turgut, E., Holzmann, T., & Sailer, K. (2013). Innovation Intermediaries: A Process View on Open Innovation Coordination. *Technology Analysis & Strategic Management, 25*, 295–309. https://doi.org/10.1080/09537325.2013.764982.

Kerry, C., & Danson, M. (2016). Open Innovation, Triple Helix and Regional Innovation Systems. *Industry and Higher Education, 30*, 67–78. https://doi.org/10.5367/ihe.2016.0292.

Kilelu, C. W., Klerkx, L., Leeuwis, C., & Hall, A. (2011). Beyond Knowledge Brokering: An Exploratory Study on Innovation Intermediaries in an Evolving

Smallholder Agricultural System in Kenya. *Knowledge Management for Development Journal, 7*, 84–108. https://doi.org/10.1080/19474199.2011.593859.

Kim, E. S. (2015). *Facilitating Innovation in SMEs: The Case of Public Intermediaries in South Korea* [Doctoral Thesis]. Edinburgh: The University of Edinburgh.

Kivimaa, P. (2014). Government-Affiliated Intermediary Organisations as Actors in System-Level Transitions. *Research Policy, 43*, 1370–1380. https://doi.org/10.1016/j.respol.2014.02.007.

Klerkx, L. and Leeuwis, C. 2008. Matching demand and supply in the agricultural knowledge infrastructure: Experiences with innovation intermediaries. *Food Policy, 33*(3): 260–276.

Klewitz, J., Zeyen, A., & Hansen, E. G. (2013). Intermediaries Driving Eco-Innovation in SMEs: A Qualitative Investigation. *European Journal of Innovation Management, 15*, 442–467. https://doi.org/10.1108/14601061211272376.

Kristjanson, P., Reid, S.R, Dickson, N., Clark, C.W., Romney, D., Puskur, R., MacMillan, R. and Grace, D. 2009. Linking international agricultural research knowledge with action for sustainable development. *Proceedings of the National Academy of Sciences, 9*(13): 1–6.

Lee, S., Park, G., Yoon, B., & Park, J. (2010). Open Innovation in SMEs-an Intermediated Network Model. *Research Policy, 39*, 290–300. https://doi.org/10.1016/j.respol.2009.12.009.

Leydesdorff, L., & Etzkowitz, H. (1995). The Triple Helix—University-Industry-Government Relations: A Laboratory for Knowledge Base Economics Development. *EASST Review, 14*, 14–19.

Löfsten, H., & Lindelöf, P. (2002). Science Parks and the Growth of New Technology-Based Firms—Academic-Industry Links, Innovation and Markets. *Research Policy, 31*, 859–876. https://doi.org/10.1016/S0048-7333(01)00153-6.

Lopez-Vega, H. (2009). How Demand-Driven Technological Systems of Innovation Work? The Role of Intermediary Organizations. In *DRUID-DIME Academy PhD Conference*.

Lukkarinen, J., Berg, A., Salo, M., Tainio, P., Alhola, K., & Antikainen, R. (2018). An Intermediary Approach to Technological Innovation Systems (TIS)—The Case of the Cleantech Sector in Finland. In *Environmental Innovation and Societal Transitions* (pp. 136–146). https://doi.org/10.1016/j.eist.2017.04.003.

Malerba, F. (2005). Sectoral Systems of Innovation: A Framework for Linking Innovation to the Knowledge Base, Structure and Dynamics of Sectors. *Economics of Innovation and New Technology, 14*, 63–82. https://doi.org/10.1080/1043859042000228688.

McEvily, B., & Zaheer, A. (1999). Bridging Ties: A Source of Firm Heterogeneity in Competitive Capabilities. *Strategic Management Journal, 20*, 1133–1156. https://doi.org/10.1002/(SICI)1097-0266(199912)20:12<1133::AID-SMJ74>3.0.CO;2-7.

Mgumia, A. H., Mattee, A. Z., & Kundi, B. A. T. (2015). Contribution of Innovation Intermediaries in Agricultural Innovation: The Case of Agricultural R&D in Tanzania. *African Journal of Science, Technology, Innovation and Development, 7*, 151–160. https://doi.org/10.1080/20421338.2015.1023644.

Mian, S. (1996). Assessing Value-Added Contributions of University Technology Business Incubators to. Tenant Firms'. *Research Policy, 25*, 325–335.

Ngwenya, H., & Hagmann, J. (2011). Making Innovation Systems Work in Practice: Experiences in Integrating Innovation, Social Learning and Knowledge in Innovation Platforms. *Knowledge Management for Development Journal, 7*, 109–124. https://doi.org/10.1080/19474199.2011.593867.

Nilsson, M., & Sia-Ljungström, C. (2013, February 18–23). The Role of Innovation Intermediaries in Innovation Systems. In *2013 International European Forum* (pp. 161–180). Innsbruck/Igls: International European Forum on System Dynamics and Innovation in Food Networks.

Nonaka, I., Reinmoeller, P., & Senoo, D. (1998). The "ART" of Knowledge: Systems to Capitalize on Market Knowledge. *European Management Journal, 16*, 673–684. https://doi.org/10.1016/S0263-2373(98)00044-9.

Nyström, A. G., Leminen, S., Westerlund, M., & Kortelainen, M. (2014). Actor Roles and Role Patterns Influencing Innovation in Living Labs. *Industrial Marketing Management, 43*, 483–495. https://doi.org/10.1016/j.indmarman.2013.12.016.

Parida, V., Westerberg, M., & Frishammar, J. (2012). Inbound Open Innovation Activities in High-Tech SMEs: The Impact on Innovation Performance. *Journal of Small Business Management, 50*, 283–309. https://doi.org/10.1111/j.1540-627X.2012.00354.x.

Pavitt, K. (2006). Innovation Processes. In J. Fagerberg, D. C. Mowery, & R. R. Nelson (Eds.), *The Oxford Handbook of Innovation*. Oxford: Oxford University Press.

Pittaway, L., Robertson, M., Munir, K., Denyer, D., & Neely, A. (2004). Networking and Innovation: A Systematic Review of the Evidence. *International Journal of Management Reviews, 5–6*, 137–168.

Pullen, A. J. J. J., De Weerd-Nederhof, P. C., Groen, A. J., & Fisscher, O. A. M. M. (2012). Open Innovation in Practice: Goal Complementarity and Closed NPD Networks to Explain Differences in Innovation Performance for SMEs in the Medical Devices Sector. *Journal of Product Innovation Management, 29*, 917–934. https://doi.org/10.1111/j.1540-5885.2012.00973.x.

Russo, M., & Rossi, F. (2009). Cooperation Networks and Innovation: A Complex Systems Perspective to the Analysis and Evaluation of a Regional Innovation Policy Programme. *Evaluation, 15*, 75–99. https://doi.org/10.1177/1356389008097872.

Sapsed, J., Grantham, A., & De Fillippi, R. (2007). A Bridge Over Troubled Waters: Bridging Organizations and Entrepreneurial Opportunities in Emerging Sectors. *Research Policy, 36*, 1314.

Simard, C., & West, J. (2006). "Knowledge networks and the geographic locus of innovation." In: Chesbrough, H., Vanhaverbeke, W., & West, J. (Eds.). (2006). *Open innovation: Researching a new paradigm.* Oxford: Oxford University Press, pp. 220–240.

Smits, R., & Kuhlmann, S. (2004). The Rise of Systemic Instruments in Innovation Policy. *International Journal of Foresight and Innovation Policy, 1*, 4. https://doi.org/10.1504/IJFIP.2004.004621.

Sun, P. Y. T., & Anderson, M. H. (2010). An Examination of the Relationship Between Absorptive Capacity and Organizational Learning, and a Proposed Integration. *International Journal of Management Reviews, 12*, 130–150. https://doi.org/10.1111/j.1468-2370.2008.00256.x.

Swann, G. M. P. (2009). *The Economics of Innovation: An Introduction, 2009.* New York: Edward Elgar Publishing. https://doi.org/10.1556/AOecon.60.2010.4.6.

Tidd, J., Bessant, J., & Pavitt, K. (2005). *Managing Innovation: Integrating Technological, Managerial Organizational Change* (3rd ed.). New York: John Wiley and Sons.

van Lente, H., Hekkert, M., Smits, R. and van Waveren, B. 2003. Roles of systemic intermediaries in transition process. International Journal of Innovation Management, 7(3): 1–33.

van de Vrande, V., De Jong, J., Vanhaverbeke, W., & de Rochemont, M. (2009). Open Innovation in SMEs: Trends, Motives and Management Challenges. *Technovation, 29*, 423–437. https://doi.org/10.1016/j.technovation.2008.10.001.

Van der Meulen, B., Nedeva, M., Braun, D., van der Meulen, B., Nedeva, M., & Braun, D. (2005). *Intermediaries Organisation and Processes: Theory and Research Issues.* PRIME Workshop.

Vidmar, M. (2019). *The "Living Lab" Method: Discovery > Challenge > Innovation.* Edinburgh. https://doi.org/10.13140/RG.2.2.21744.20484.

Vidmar, M., Rosiello, A., Williams, R., Vermeulen, N., & Dines, J. (2020). New Space and Agile Innovation: Understanding Transition to Open Innovation Through Examining Innovation Networks and Moments. *Acta Astronautica, 167*, 122–134.

Von Tunzelmann, N. (2009). Competencies Versus Capabilities: A Reassessment. *Economics and Politics, 26*, 435–464. https://doi.org/10.1428/30999.

Vonortas, N. S. (2002). Building Competitive Firms: Technology Policy Initiatives in Latin America. *Technology in Society, 24*, 433–459. https://doi.org/10.1016/S0160-791X(02)00034-9.

Wang, J. (2018). Innovation and Government Intervention: A Comparison of Singapore and Hong Kong. *Research Policy, 47*, 399–412. https://doi.org/10.1016/j.respol.2017.12.008.

West, J., & Bogers, M. (2014). Leveraging External Sources of Innovation: A Review of Research on Open Innovation. *Journal of Product Innovation Management, 31*, 814–831. https://doi.org/10.1111/jpim.12125.

Winch, G. M., & Courtney, R. (2007). The Organization of Innovation Brokers: An International Review. *Technology Analysis & Strategic Management, 19*, 747–763. https://doi.org/10.1080/09537320701711223.

Zahra, S. A., & George, G. (2002). Absorptive Capacity: A Review, Reconceptualization, and Extension. *The Academy of Management Review, 27*, 185–203. https://doi.org/10.5465/AMR.2002.6587995.

CHAPTER 3

Innovation Intermediaries and the "Final Frontier" of the New Space Sector in Scotland

Abstract This chapter presents the empirical case study of the macro-level landscape and micro-level roles and activities of innovation intermediaries in the emergent New Space sector in Scotland. This is based on a mix of industrial/innovation policy document analysis, social-network mapping and case studies with survey data. The wealth of thus collected empirical evidence makes clear the need for a holistic approach to innovation support policy and its operationalisation.

Keywords New Space sector • Scotland • Innovation intermediaries • Landscape mapping • Policy • Geo-sectoral innovation landscape

To better understand the role of innovation intermediaries within the emergent New Space sector in Scotland, the structure of the sector itself needs to be examined. From innovation studies' point of view, the Space Sector analysis is split into three main value chain segments: upstream—hardware (satellite) manufacturing and (rocket) launch infrastructure; mid-stream—operational deployment in space and data downlink; and downstream—data analysis and information services (Adlen 2011; OECD 2007; Satellite Applications Catapult 2014). The activities of the sector link up to other industrial value chains, in particular advance manufacturing, electronics and information technologies. In addition, as most high-tech sectors, Space Sector businesses also depend on the availability of

M. Vidmar, *Innovation Intermediaries and (Final) Frontiers of High-tech*, https://doi.org/10.1007/978-3-030-60642-8_3

low-tech components and non-specialist services. Nonetheless, the Space value chain covers such an extensive ground as to render it particularly comprehensive research field. This gives rise to an opportunity to study inter-organisational dynamics and innovation processes spanning the development of advance materials/composites, through systems engineering, and all the way to software design.

The industry is currently undergoing a major transition from "Classic Space Industry" to "New Space" (Adlen 2011). This is specifically related to cheaper electronics technology bringing down cost of satellite manufacturing, expanded free access to space data from public programmes, as well as cloud-based platforms for operation and data management. The New Space applications markets are primarily expanding in Earth Observation domain, that is analysis of satellite images, though the only really profitable Space Industry market so far was telecommunications/broadcasting. This is reflected in new initiatives as well, such as One Web (Caleb 2016) and Starlink (Freeman 2020) constellations—bringing worldwide broadband using thousands of small and cheap nano satellites. In all, the significant amount of existing growth in the wider Space Sector led to an increasing economic and political interest. Furthermore, these developments allowed traditionally peripheral places, such as Scotland, to emerge as new powerhouses.

Since 2010, Scotland has slowly been gaining pace as a leader within the New Space Industry (Macdonald 2017, 2019). Particular areas of excellence are in nano-sat platform development and space-data driven applications (Scottish Enterprise 2016). Since the UK has led and successfully capitalised on previous Space Industry transition, as the UK was the first country to commercialise its launch capability and had a lead role in commercialising space applications especially the satellite (TV) broadcasting (Willetts 2013), policy interest in this area is also growing.[1] This aligns to wider policy agenda of support for innovation as way to generate return on investment in UK's extensive research base (Autio 2014).

[1] UK policy has been shaped by the Space Industry Growth Strategy vision and action plans (Space IGS 2011, 2014) and the "Case for Space" reports (London Economics 2009, 2015a), progress against which gets captured in the biannual "The Size and Health of UK Space Industry" survey (London Economics 2014, 2016, 2019; Oxford Economics 2010, 2012). Thus set and government-backed policy aims to see an increase of the UK share of the global Space Industry market from 7% to 10% by 2030 (Space IGS 2011, 2014; Willetts 2013) with Scottish Enterprise and Scottish Government hoping to attract 10% of that to Scotland (London Economics 2015b; Scottish Enterprise 2016).

One of the key challenges of these policy ambitions are their reliance on establishment of new enterprises. In line with general (UK) government policy, this is projected at an arm's length through innovation support, rather than through direct intervention. Particular targets for improvement through such support are entrepreneurial and venture capital climate and expansion of knowledge transfer from basic and applied research to enable the development of private-sector-driven products. Consequently, policymakers are focusing their attention mostly into supporting actors exploiting niche opportunities and consequently to the early stages of business development (UK Space Agency 2014a).

There seems to be some evidence in support of this approach. Strong inter-disciplinary tradition embodied by "city campuses" of Scottish universities has led to clusters of R&D activities emerging. Electronics research at the University of Dundee led to the development of a small communication cluster there, engineering heritage on the Clyde and the University of Strathclyde's very active Aerospace department hurried along the development of a nano-satellite manufacturing in Glasgow, and a string of spin-offs from the Schools of Geoscience and Informatics in Edinburgh has led to a world-renowned Earth Observation data analytics applications cluster. The dispersed yet loosely aligned Space Industry in Scotland is often referred to the Agile Space or the "Space Glen" triangle (Vidmar 2020).[2] Hence, public funding is being invested in a series of initiatives to help facilitate knowledge and technology spill-over (Autio et al. 2004; Salter and Martin 2001). Specific interest in supporting such endeavours is focused on innovation intermediaries—which currently enjoy a high degree of innovation policy interest across the high-tech sectors (Dalziel 2010; Howells 2006) and in the Space Sector in particular (Comstock and Lockney 2007; Petroni et al. 2013; Venturini and Verbano 2014).

As an example, the Satellite Applications Catapult and the UK Space Agency were both established within this period, alongside the consolidation of the national R&D and innovation agency, Innovate UK and the research councils, now all joined into UK Research and Innovation (UKRI). In Scotland, these organisations are joined by the Scottish Government's regional economic development agencies, in particular the

[2] Slightly less relevant locales due to their low innovation rate and/or relative short track record are the proposed sites of spaceports, that is small rockets launch sites, in the North of Scotland and the space-based maritime services supporting North Sea off-shore industries out of ports in Aberdeenshire.

Scottish Space Innovation Intermediation Landscape

European Space Agency (ESA) is an international organisation for space exploration, which includes member states from Europe and beyond. It operates a network of research centres across Europe and many manned and unmanned missions including extensive projects such as European Union (EU)-backed development of the new global navigation satellite system, Galileo, and Earth Observation services, Copernicus. As part of its core mission, it is investing in technology transfer and business growth, which it stimulates by commercialising its intellectual property, supporting a series of business incubators and running competitions for entrepreneurs. In the UK, ESA has a research centre, **European Centre for Satellite Applications and Telecommunications** (**ECSAT**) in Harwell, whilst also supporting pan-UK Science and Technology Facilities Council (STFC)-run series of business incubators **ESA BIC UK** and a network of **ESA Business Application Ambassadors**. Furthermore, through the Galileo and Copernicus programmes, ESA runs a series of entrepreneurship development competitions, such as the **Galileo Masters** and **Copernicus Masters**.

UK Space Agency is the UK government's executive agency with the remit of coordinating government activities in the Space Sector. It is primarily set up to fund and steer programmes related to UK participation in international space exploration, developing new UK missions and commercialising space technology. The UK Space Agency also coordinates the **Space for Smarter Government** programme, which aims to "unlock the potential of space to enhance public sector services and reduce costs" (UK Space Agency 2014a) as well as backing incubation facilities developed by partner organisations (UK Space Agency 2017).

Innovate UK is the UK government agency promoting innovation and growth, part of UK Research and Innovation group. Developed from the Technology Strategy Board, it administers funding for R&D and business development, particularly in high-tech sectors. It is providing most of the funding for the current development of the network of technology transfer centres, called **Catapults** (including the Satellite Applications Catapult), and the **Knowledge Transfer Network** (KTN) (which also has a space section). **SatelliteApplications Catapult** is an independent innovation and technology development company, created by the Innovate UK to foster growth across the economy through the exploitation of space data. They provide technical and business support, including access to facilities, and work to integrate and promote Space Sector. They operate a series of regional centres, which they established through a competitive bidding programme, including the **Scottish Centre of Excellence in Satellite Applications (SoXA),** at the University of Strathclyde.

Science and Technology Facilities Council (STFC) is also part of the UK Research and Innovation (UKRI) family of funding and support agencies developing academic and applied research in the UK. Two other research councils also have a significant stake in the Space Sector, namely Engineering and Physical Sciences Research Council (EPSRC), which is supporting the development of advanced materials and engineering solutions for space exploration, and Natural Environment Research Council (NERC), which is supporting the development of applications in Earth Observation (EO). **UK Astronomy Technology Centre (UK ATC)** is the only STFC research facility in Scotland, based at the **Royal Observatory Edinburgh (ROE).** They specialise in building infra-red detectors, data pipelines for microwave and radio telescopes, and complex systems engineering. **ATC Innovations** is the commercialisation arm of UK ATC, tasked with technology transfer and business relationships, including the new **Higgs Centre for Innovation,** comprising an ESA and UK Space Agency backed business incubator. The other main space-related STFC facility is the space arm of the Rutherford-Appleton Laboratory in Harwell (near Oxford in England), the **RAL Space**.

Scottish Enterprise (SE) is an executive agency of Scottish government, tasked to develop businesses in Scotland under the devolved administration, with particular remit over the Central Belt (SE and SW Scotland). Its key objective is support for new venture creation, business development and growth (particularly in exports). SE coordinates the activities of several regional trade-association/chamber-of-commerce-like bodies, including Aerospace, Defence, Marine and Security Industry Leadership Group, now also with a separate affiliate **Scottish Space Leadership Council**, which acts on

(*continued*)

(continued)

behalf of the Space Sector. SE works in close partnership with **Scottish Development International (SDI)**, the Scottish government agency tasked with inward investment and the **Highlands and Islands Enterprise (HIE)**, SE's sister agency with the remit in the North of Scotland and particularly active in the development of spaceports.

UK Space is a trade association for businesses operating in the Space Sector in the UK. It plays a significant role in shaping the **Space Innovation and Growth Strategy (Space IGS)**, which is the key government-backed initiative to develop the sector. The establishment of the UK Space Agency and the prominent role Space Sector has in the UK government's economic growth policies are based on this initiative. There are many key international players with crucial infrastructure in the UK and some in Scotland. In particular, the UK has several of the core **Airbus, Finmeccanica** and **Thales** space-related subsidiaries and facilities, with part of the multi-national corporation **Leonardo**, a defence business with some space-related products being located in Edinburgh. There are also a number of large UK firms with a significant space portfolio, such as **QinetiQ, BAE Systems** and **e2v**.

Universities in the UK have a longstanding tradition of excellence in research in natural sciences, including space exploration. In Scotland, **Universities** of **Dundee, Strathclyde** and **Edinburgh** have the most significant research programmes in this area, in electronics, systems engineering and data applications, respectively. There are a wider variety of consultancy and commercialisation efforts on behalf of these universities, in particular through spin-out and knowledge transfer programmes. There is also a series of technology incubators in Scotland, for example, Edinburgh-based **CodeBase, TechCube**, the **Science Triangle** and **Alba Innovation** (in Livingston), all of which take in companies with space-related innovations.

Central Scotland's Scottish Enterprise. Among them these organisations funded several key projects, for example, the first UK-built cube-sat, UKube-1 (Macdonald and Lowe 2014). In addition, significant investment in business incubation facilities (Satellite Applications Catapult 2019; UK Space Agency 2017) and R&D/technology transfer support (UK Space Agency 2019) has been made. UKRI, too, are expanding their space-related technology transfer programmes including European Space Agency (ESA)-backed Business Incubation Centres (BIC) (Astropreneurs 2018; Banks 2018). Scottish Enterprise has also invested in networking efforts, with over £200k investment in establishing an integrated network of space-related activities (Vass 2013). These and other intermediation activities will be mapped and explored further in the next section.

Innovation Intermediaries and the New Space in Scotland

Building on in-depth participatory action research within this ecosystem, a comprehensive list of the key innovation intermediation actors active in this arena in the UK, and specifically in Scotland, has been drawn up, summarised in the box below. As is clear from this analysis, many are nested into other organisations, so the core support can be traced back to a small set of funding sources with a significant policy agenda. Thus, understanding their roles and effect on the ground is vital for successful further development.

Furthermore, when using ego-centric Social Network Analysis (ego-SNA) to build a composite picture of the Scottish New Space innovation network, innovation intermediaries turned out to be the key network integrators as the most well-connected, and hence most central, players (Vidmar 2021; Vidmar et al. 2020). This makes understanding the systemic nature of their activities imperative from the policy point of view (Fig. 3.1).

The data show that space agencies occupy the core of the Scottish New Space sector's innovation network, followed closely by a series of government-backed innovation and research agencies and universities.[3]

[3] With a notable exception of a few large multinational corporations and lead SMEs, most core network actors (noted) are public bodies, mainly innovation intermediaries. In-degree centrality (i.e. number of other actors connected to them) for Scottish New Space innovation network's secondary nodes, filtered to show public actors with multiple edges (links) only: European Space Agency (ESA)—11; Scottish Enterprise—8; UK Space Agency—8; Satellite

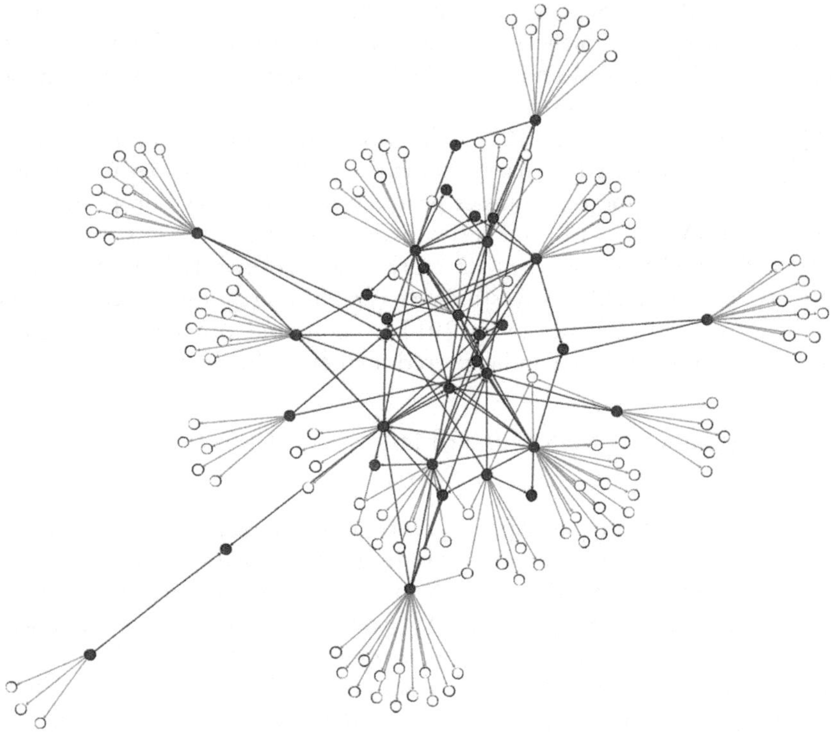

Fig. 3.1 Scottish New Space SMEs' innovation network, plotted with Gephi (0.9.2) software using Hu's proportional algorithm (Hu 2005). The colours are highlighting the originating ego-centric SMEs (nodes marked in blue) and the innovation intermediaries, research centres and governmental agencies (marked in red). (Source: Vidmar 2021)

There are only a limited number of private organisations at the core of this network, which are heavily based on knowledge exchange, as per the previously outlined policy framework. Hence, understanding its dynamic is vital for sectoral and broader economic development as well as learning

Applications Catapult—6; Innovate UK—6; University of Edinburgh—5; University of Strathclyde—4; Scottish Centre of Excellence in Satellite Applications (SoXA)—3; Space Network Scotland—3; RAL Space—2; NASA—2; DLR (German Space Agency)—2; UK government—2; Data Lab—2; University of Leicester—2; Scottish government—2; Heriot-Watt University—2.

lessons about support for high-tech industries in the era of reaching for the "endless frontiers" of technology (Bush 1945) and the specific perception of space technology as the "final" frontier (Genta and Rycroft 2003). However, as pointed out earlier, the somewhat complex and confusing nature of intermediaries roles and functions is making it difficult to develop a clear picture of what activities are provided and if there is any type of support that is missing.

Roles of Innovation Intermediaries Within the Scottish New Space Sector

As outlined in the previous section, the Scottish New Space innovation network seems to be centrally integrated around a cluster of innovation intermediaries. Apart from the European and UK space agencies, the most centrally integrated local organisations seem to derive from the support frameworks put in place by the Scottish and UK governments. The governments fund a series of initiatives, most notably the respective economic development and science and technology funding agencies, the Scottish Enterprise and the UK Research and Innovation (UKRI). In turn, these organisations fund on-the-ground initiatives, such as grant investment funding, knowledge exchange and business support networks, and business incubation and acceleration programmes. Specifically, the four interventions examined in the next four subsections illustrate how:

- Scottish Enterprise's flagship SMART: SCOTLAND awards have provided capital investment for specific projects, whilst the wider programme helped develop skills and capacities.
- UKRI/STFC's Higgs Centre for Innovation is offering physical space and equipment to emerging companies to accelerate their R&D.
- With Scottish Space Symposia and Data.Space conferences, the Scottish Centre of Excellence in Satellite Applications brought together most of the Scottish New Space sector to discuss and develop a common vision.
- The UKube-1 project led by UK Space Agency provided a critical opportunity to develop some of the Scottish New Space SMEs to become global leaders in cube-sat technology.

SMART Awards and Scottish Space Network (by Scottish Enterprise)

The SMART: SCOTLAND awards is a funding and business development and promotion scheme, delivered by the Scottish Government's regional economic development agencies, chiefly the one responsible for Central Scotland, the Scottish Enterprise (Scottish Enterprise 2019). The SMART: Scotland award has been won by several lead SMEs in the Scottish New Space sector since the early 2000s. In particular, STAR Dundee, a University of Dundee spin-off working with on-board satellite communications, has won two SMART awards in 2002 and 2006 respectively. However, so did the more recently established Clyde Space, a nano-satellite manufacturer and integration firm (in 2006 and 2017), as well as the latest New Space generation firms, for instance, Alba Orbital, for their own, even smaller (pico-) satellite and components development (in 2014); and to the incoming US-originating space-enabled asset tracking SME, Spire (in 2015). These awards are critical in the context of enabling the development of applied R&D and are focusing mainly on upstream segments of various high-tech industries. In particular, the scheme itself describes its mission as helping

> *undertake technical feasibility studies and research and development (R&D) projects that have a commercial endpoint.* (Scottish Enterprise 2019)

The SMART: SCOTLAND offers feasibility studies funding of up to £100k (expecting a minimum of 30–40% match funding from SMEs) and R&D project funding of up to £600k (with 65% match funding from SMEs). These non-refundable grants are awarded through a competitive process through which SMEs:

> *must be able to demonstrate:*
>
> - *That you own, or have rights to exploit, the intellectual property required to undertake the project*
> - *All intellectual property developed throughout the project will be owned by the company receiving grant funding*
> - *How commercial prospects for the end product or process will be achieved, with realistic and effective routes to market*
> - *That you have the necessary management and technical expertise and resources (either in-house or brought-in) to make the project a success*
> - *That both the project and the business are financially viable*
> - *That financial assistance from SMART:Scotland is essential.* (Scottish Enterprise 2019)

This is related to the programme's five aims, identified as:

- *assist small and medium-sized enterprises (SMEs) to research, develop and exploit new, technically innovative, products with good commercial potential;*
- *stimulate technical innovation and encourage best practice throughout business.*
- *strengthen the scientific and technological bases of industry;*
- *improve the future competitiveness of the Scottish economy by supporting technically innovative SMEs, recognising that these are a dynamic source of new wealth creation, employment and export sales; and*
- *help contribute towards a climate which encourages investment in innovative technology by individuals, companies and financial institutions and which stimulates a market in technological advancement.* (Boyns et al. 2009, p. 9)

Hence, SMART: SCOTLAND scheme is not only providing the necessary funding but also encouraging the development of skills in innovation and business capacity. In a report evaluating the first ten years of the scheme's operation (1999–2008), the authors note that:

> *large majorities of grant recipients acknowledged that they had: improved their innovation culture; become better able to manage innovation; improved their innovation/technical understanding; and, invested more in innovation in general.* (Boyns et al. 2009, p. 7)

The Scottish Enterprise also provides additional targeted business development support, including coordinating unified Scottish exhibition spaces at industry conferences, as well as funding a dedicated knowledge brokerage and business network development initiative, called the Space Network Scotland (SNS), established in 2014. Whilst SMART: SCOTLAND awards target capital investment in specific key technology development areas, the SNS is enabling the translation of interests across the sector and more widely into the economy, as well as more efficient sharing of resources. A surveyed partner in the programme noted:

> *Space Network Scotland was created to provide a focal point and a resource for Scotland's space sector. Key to its activities is the identification and creation of opportunities.*

Mentioning also that these "are the areas where there is a provision that can be most beneficial at relatively low cost" as they explained that

> *This focus came initially from discussions that Scottish Enterprise had with space companies in Scotland, was refined by the expertise of the SNS staff, and then further refined by feedback from industry following work that we undertook.*

In particular, a recent internal review of the SNS work argued that:

> *The overall conclusions from the questionnaire were that:*
>
> - *Most interest in support came from respondents who see themselves entirely or largely as space organisations.*
> - *The priority interests of the sector are representation to government, marketing of the sector and networking events.*
> - *Promoting Scottish capability in new space was equally popular with promoting space capability more broadly.*
> - *Only around half of the companies that responded are currently members of a trade body.*
>
> *At the follow-on meeting the broad consensus was that support should continue to be light touch and response to the companies and universities that make up the network.* (Space Network Scotland 2017)

Higgs Centre for Innovation (by Science and Technology Facilities Council)

Higgs Centre for Innovation in Edinburgh is part of the effort to spread the reach of Science and Technology Facilities Council's (part of UKRI) support for innovation to Scotland (STFC 2013). Though the initiative predates it, its public announcement coincided with the award of Nobel Prize in Physics to the Edinburgh-based theoretical physicist, Peter Higgs. The project strives to create a regional incubator, thematically aligned to the local research strengths, in particular in particle physics and astronomy and space technology, closely linked to STFC's UK Astronomical Technology Centre, based at the Royal Observatory Edinburgh. In Autumn of 2013, the plans for this new intermediary were announced in a press release as:

> A new Higgs Centre for Innovation announced today (5 December 2013) aims to create new market opportunities whilst also inspiring the next generation of scientists and engineers. [...] [which] *will apply business incubation best practice to big data and space technology, enabling start-ups to translate fundamental research into wider commercial impact.* (STFC 2013)

In order to deliver on this mandate, the centre was designed to:

- *House and incubate up to 12 high-tech start-up businesses*
- *Support them with a comprehensive package of business training, technical advice, and access to equipment and facilities*
- *Provide PhD students with direct experience of entrepreneurial environments*
- *Offer to SMEs access to specialist labs and test facilities for micro/nano-satellites housed within dedicated clean-rooms*

Furthermore,

> *The BIC is part of the European Space Agency (ESA) BIC UK*, CERN BIC, and UK Space Agency (UKSA) BIC networks.* (STFC 2018)

As well as it is being run in partnership with the University of Edinburgh.

Crucially, this type of intervention requires significant financial investment and is difficult to establish without a pre-existing emergent ecosystem—including a critical mass of companies—and a significant social capital, most often built on past track record and/or existing infrastructure. In this case, this manifests as:

> *The Science and Technology Facilities Council (STFC) received a capital investment of £10.7M from the Treasury to construct the new centre. STFC will invest £2M over five years to operate the centre.* (STFC 2013)

And

> *The new centre will build on the success and proven track record of similar models seen in the STFC ESA and CERN Business Incubation Centres as well as the Innovations Technology Access Centre.*

The centre construction was opened in May 2018. Crucially, due to the significant amount of public funding involved in this project, the steering vision for the centre is far more modest, in line with the technological neutrality conceptualisation of allowing for open competition instead of pre-determining priority technologies, also referred to as "picking winners" (Azar and Sandén 2011). Also of note is the extensive start-up and spin-out focus, engaging with the early-stage innovation process and emerging opportunities and markets. As expressed by the surveyed member of Higgs Centre for Innovation staff, their aim is "to make links between academic research and the commercial world".

In particular, there is a lack of access to specialised equipment and physical space, as well as more targeted activities to disperse knowledge and skills. Hence, emerging organically from industry demand and public policy supply, the Higgs Centre for Innovation was designed to fill this gap of equipping the emerging sectoral players.

Scottish Space Symposium and Data.Space (by Scottish Centre of Excellence in Satellite Applications)

The Scottish New Space sector has developed organically mainly in three distinct clusters, with extensive expertise in space data applications hosted in Edinburgh, space hardware developers based in Glasgow and a small number of sub-systems developers (mainly in electronics and embedded software) in Dundee (Vidmar 2020). Though these disparate clusters mainly grew and developed separately, various actors in the industry realised that a level of integration across the sector and region would be desirable as a bulwark against market fluctuations. In order to assist in this vertical value chain integration and to create a unique selling point of Scotland being one-stop-shop for New Space solutions, a group at Strathclyde University, in partnership with their key contacts in the industry, has been developing a series of interventions to facilitate cross-sector interaction and regional coordination. In 2014 they also applied to host the Scottish Centre of Excellence in Satellite Applications (SoXSA). This is part of the UK-wide network of centres of excellence in the Space Sector, all linked to the Satellite Application Catapult, one of the main nodes in the "Catapult" network of innovation centres overseen by the UK government's innovation agency, Innovate UK. The SoXSA have engaged in a variety of programmes, both national (through their parent Catapult) as well as regionally and locally, for more targeted project work and support for key partners. A highlight of the local programme is the establishment of a small incubation programme in partnership with Glasgow-based Tontine incubator and funded from UK Space Agency, which

> *will support six companies for an incubation period of one year. Throughout the incubation period, the companies will benefit from superb accommodation, unparalleled business support and access to a wide business network through SoXSA*. (Tontine 2018)

However, the wider regional programme is of most interest, as it created on promoting a new dynamic in the Space Sector in Scotland, a cross-sectoral regional integration. The surveyed member of SoXSA team noted that:

> *We aim to be "Scotland's place in space", building and supporting the space network, and generating high value projects to develop the sector and the Scottish economy*. [...] We focus on connecting academia, industry and innovation centres etc. to make the right people engage to benefit Scotland economically and otherwise.

These activities were particularly brought to the fore in their pivotal role to assist meeting and networking in the sector, by running a series of Scottish Space Symposia (2010, 2012, 2015 and 2017), leading to more recently organising an annual Data.Space conference (2017, 2018) with international reach. Scottish Space Symposia were explicitly designed to develop a community of actors in this emerging sector and engage in sector promotion. This description was used in the announcement of the 1st Scottish Space Symposium in 2010:

> *Scotland is emerging as an international centre for a range of disruptive new space technologies. While this growing industrial and academic capability is recognised in sectors of the space industry, the profile of this capability needs to be raised in Scotland. In addition, the potential of Scotland to continue to grow in the space sector needs to be unlocked by developing a strong sense of community and reaching out to industry and university groups who do not yet recognise the opportunities space can provide*. (1st Scottish Space Symposium—University of Strathclyde 2010)

In particular, the event was designed to provide:

> *An opportunity to network with the Scottish space technology community*

> *A forum to identify key capabilities, future partnerships and opportunities*
> *A platform to raise the profile of the Scottish space technology community.*
> (1st Scottish Space Symposium—University of Strathclyde 2010)

This mandate was carried over and expanded to an international level when Data.Space was announced. In particular, it was centred on

> *bring[ing] together data users from across the economy with data generators from the space sector as well as pooling innovators and entrepreneurs from academia and the commercial sector with regulators, legislators and venture capitalists.* (Satellite Applications Catapult 2014)

Both of the events had a very successful run and the ideas behind the value chain integration resulted in the establishment of the Agile Space group, a loose industry consortium, which was announced at Data.Space 2017, though it has not become fully active yet. Similarly, the concept of regional integration has received attention by the Scottish Government Industry Leadership Group (on Defence, Marine, Security and Aerospace) in their 2016 Strategy, with a special sub-committee for Scottish Space Industry Action Plan being formed at the time, now called the Scottish Space Leadership Council (SSLC). These activities and ideas framed the development of the Space Sector in Scotland "brand", with a unique selling point related to regional competitive advantage. The branding is focusing on Scotland becoming the "one-stop-shop" for (new) space solutions with partner companies producing hardware, launching payloads, operating space assets, collecting data and extracting information for the customer. Though several components of the value chain are still in development (in particular the launch capability), this image of Scotland as a key "space hub" has gained political and economic traction within and outwith the sector (Vidmar 2019), now championed by the SSLC.

UKube-1 (by UK Space Agency)

From the perspective of several lead players, a key transformational project in the Scottish New Space sector was the UKube-1 project, a tender to design, build, launch and operate the first UK cube-sat. A cube-sat is a nano-satellite platform build of cube units (10-10-10 cm), weighing a few kilograms (ESA 2019). They were initially developed as training and outreach kits, though once several units (3+) are stuck together, they create a bus capable of meaningful space deployment. These cube-sats are one of the key innovations powering the New Space era of space exploration and industry, as their small size, enabled by miniaturisation of consumer electronics, and low cost (by using off-the-shelf components) enabled radically new technological solutions reaching a completely new market. In particular, their low cost and modular architecture make them almost "disposable" and in a low earth orbit location, their 18-month lifespan is short enough that the components need no radiation protection, making the craft lighter and hence the launch significantly cheaper. The low cost and industrial-scale modular integration are also enabling mass production of cube-sats, leading to the creation of constellations (i.e. several satellites orbiting the Earth in formation), where tasks can be distributed and revisit rates (flypast over the same area on the Earth's surface) can be high, that is enabling near real-time data capture from space.

UK Space Agency led the UKube-1 project with the explicit intention of producing a technology demonstrator as a precursor to commercialising domestic cube-sat capability. The surveyed project participant noted that the main objective of UKube-1 was built around the "need to establish and develop upstream space capability in Scotland and UK". In particular, there was a good opportunity to "use cost-effective CubeSat missions to achieve this" and then leading to "provide further offerings with high export potential". The initial idea for this project arose from academic research, supported by Knowledge Transfer Partnership scheme, between Strathclyde University and Clyde Space, then a leading developer of high-performance space-ready batteries, who wanted to expand their business in this interesting new technology area. Funding has been sought from the Scottish government on a similar project called ScotSAT, but financial constraints of the post-economic crash era meant that the proposal was not successful. This is how UKube-1's stakeholders are described by the UK government:

> *UKube-1 is an exciting and novel collaboration between the UK Space Agency, industry and academia. The funding partners for UKube-1 are the UK Space Agency, the Technology Strategy Board and STFC. The spacecraft is being developed through a Knowledge Transfer Partnership with innovative Scottish company Clyde Space and the University of Strathclyde, supported with internal funding from Clyde Space. The UK's largest space company, EADS Astrium Ltd, is providing engineering and programme management support to the Agency for the pilot programme. UK industry and academia are provid-*

ing the payloads and the ground support operations and the launch will be procured by the UK Space Agency. (UK Space Agency 2014b)

Crucially, as noted in the text, the project was of interest to big space players as well (especially EADS Astrium, a large aerospace and defence multinational corporation), who leveraged their influence through the then newly created UK Space Agency, to interest the government in this opportunity—the project participant surveyed stressed that "use of lobbying and ministerial level support was critical". Building on a pre-existing consortium of national players, in particular academics interested to send instruments in space, and tapping into the contemporary political interest in innovation and the emergence of New Space trends, the core players involved in the feasibility studies (EADS Astrium, Strathclyde University and Clyde Space), pitched an optimistic mission plan to launch UKube-1 as a transformative opportunity for the UK Space Industry and consequently the UK economy. The surveyed UKube-1 participant, in particular, stressed the importance of

buy-in from Astrium, who then supported us to engage with BNSC [British National Space Centre] and get [their] CEO [a] seat on the space leadership council.

The programme was then run by the UK Space Agency with the very specific mandate (as noted in the quoted UK government briefing above) and in a very hands-on manner, though funding was quite limited for most of the project. The participant mentioned some of these limitations specifically, noting that "while more knowledge might have been useful, the costs would likely have been prohibitive".

Overall, this intervention, which involved an investment of capital and direct project work:

helped maintain the UK's leading position in the CubeSat sector. Participation in the mission placed Clyde Space in an excellent position to capitalise on the fast-growing global nanosatellite market. The company has experienced 100% year on year growth, both in turnover and employees, as a direct result from involvement in UKube-1, and is firmly established as a global leader. (UK Space Agency 2015)

The effect of this was particularly strongly felt in Scotland, where the lead developers, Clyde Space, are based. The intention was also to translate this opportunity to a wider community of New Space subsystems and payload developers, which partially materialised, in particular for the Dundee-based on-board software developers Bright Ascension and the academic partners, Strathclyde University. These partnerships by and large endure and importantly add to the development of the Scottish New Space sector by continuing R&D and access to specific markets.

Towards Systematisation of Scottish New Space Innovation Intermediation

The landscape mapping and detailed case studies of the lead innovation intermediaries' interventions outlined above have framed the variety of roles intermediaries (can) play in innovation systems. However, not only do they extend beyond, or rather outside, many of the analysed classifications from Chap. 2, they are also often spanning several of the categories. Example here is the Higgs Centre for Innovation, which at once provides physical space for start-up businesses, but also sees themselves as knowledge and technology brokers. How do we analytically deal with these boundary spanning organisations? Moreover, if such empirical studies are to identify the optimal additional provision—how can a mix of activities and resource provisions be assessed and new/additional interventions advised?

There are evolutionary processes at play as well—Scottish Enterprise initial investment in competitive funding was later supplemented by a targeted intervention in support of sectoral networking and integration. Though evolutionary pathways have been extensively researched within the dominant knowledge brokerage intermediary roles and some of the associated R&D and co-design (Hakkarainen and Hyysalo 2016; Kilelu et al. 2011) less clarity exists when other provisions are included, such as provision of equipment and skills (like in the case of Higgs Centre for Innovation), sector integration (like the work of SoXSA and SNS) or effects of deployment of capital (as was seen in the case of UKube-1).

Hence, another look at the available insights from the state-of-the-art literature is needed in order to map out the systemic landscape of innovation intermediation interventions. Analysing where the boundaries are drawn and why may help explain the reasons for the boundary spanning organisations as well as frame a classification of their activities, which will allow for identified combinations of interventions, including the mix of neutral and competitive capital investment and targeted networking support. In the next chapter, such a classification, as well as accompanying contextual reasons/factors, and the emerging organisational typology are developed.

Bibliography

1st Scottish Space Symposium—University of Strathclyde [WWW Document]. (2010). https://www.strath.ac.uk/advancedspaceconceptslaboratory/news-events/scottishspacesymposia/1stscottishspacesymposium/. Accessed 24 Dec 2018.

Adlen, S. (2011). *Innovation in the Global Space Industry*. London: Imperial College London.

Astropreneurs. (2018). An Interview with the European Space Agency (ESA's) Business Incubation Centre (BIC) UK [WWW Document]. Astropreneurs. http://astropreneurs.space/2019/02/07/an-interview-with-the-european-space-agency-esas-business-incubation-centre-bic-uk/. Accessed 1 Apr 2019.

Autio, E. (2014). *Innovation from Big Science: Enhancing Big Science Impact Agenda*. London: Department of Business, Innovation and Skill.

Autio, E., Hameri, A. P., & Vuola, O. (2004). A Framework of Industrial Knowledge Spillovers in Big-Science Centers. *Research Policy, 33*, 107–126. https://doi.org/10.1016/S0048-7333(03)00105-7.

Azar, C., & Sandén, B. A. (2011). The Elusive Quest for Technology-Neutral Policies. *Environmental Innovation and Societal Transitions, 1*, 135–139. https://doi.org/10.1016/j.eist.2011.03.003.

Banks, M. (2018). UK Space Sector Set for Take-Off. *Physics World, 31*, 13–13. https://doi.org/10.1088/2058-7058/31/7/20.

Boyns, N., Spires, R., & Cox, M. (2009). *Evaluation of Smart: Scotland*. Edinburgh: Scottish Government Social Research.

Bush, V. (1945). *Science: The Endless Frontier*. Washington, DC: United States Government Printing Office.

Caleb, H. (2016). OneWeb Gets $1.2 Billion in SoftBank-Led Investment. *Sp. News*.

Comstock, D. A., & Lockney, D. (2007). NASA's Legacy of Technology Transfer and Prospects for Future Benefits. In *A Collection of Technical Papers—AIAA Space 2007 Conference* (pp. 2969–2978). https://doi.org/10.2514/6.2007-6283.

Dalziel, M. (2010). Why Do Innovation Intermediaries Exist? In *Druid 2010: Opening Up Innovation: Strategy, Organization and Technology* (p. 23). London: Imperial College London Business School.

ESA. (2019). UKube-1 (United Kingdom Universal Bus Experiment 1) [WWW Document]. eoPortal Dir. https://earth.esa.int/web/eoportal/satellite-missions/u/ukube-1. Accessed 10 May 2019.

Freeman, R. H. (2020). Overview: Satellite Constellations. *Journal of Space Operations & Communicator, 17(2).*

Genta, G., & Rycroft, M. (2003). *Space, the Final Frontier?* Cambridge: Cambridge University Press.

Hakkarainen, L., & Hyysalo, S. (2016). The Evolution of Intermediary Activities: Broadening the Concept of Facilitation in Living Labs. *Technology Innovation Management Review, 6*, 45–58.

Howells, J. (2006). Intermediation and the Role of Intermediaries in Innovation. *Research Policy, 35*, 715–728. https://doi.org/10.1016/j.respol.2006.03.005.

Hu, Y. (2005). Efficient, High-Quality Force-Directed Graph Drawing. *Mathematica Journal, 10*, 37–71.

Kilelu, C. W., Klerkx, L., Leeuwis, C., & Hall, A. (2011). Beyond Knowledge Brokering: An Exploratory Study on Innovation Intermediaries in an Evolving Smallholder Agricultural System in Kenya. *Knowledge Management for Development Journal, 7*, 84–108. https://doi.org/10.1080/19474199.2011.593859.

London Economics. (2009). *The Case for Space 2009.* London.

London Economics. (2014). *The Size and Health of UK Space Industry.* London.

London Economics. (2015a). *The Case for Space 2015.* London: Economics.

London Economics. (2015b). *Development of the Scottish Space Industry.* Edinburgh.

London Economics. (2016). *The Size and Health of the UK Space Industry 2016.* London.

London Economics. (2019). *Size and Health of the UK Space Industry 2018.* London.

Macdonald, K. (2017). Scottish Space Industry Soaring High [WWW Document]. *BBC News.* http://www.bbc.co.uk/news/38804310

Macdonald, M. (2019). State of the Scottish Nation's Space Sector. In *Proceedings of NSSC.* Edinburgh.

Macdonald, M., & Lowe, C. J. (2014). It's Hip to Be Square: The CubeSat Revolution. *Aerospace*, 22–25.

OECD. (2007). *The Space Economy at a Glance.* OECD Publishing. https://doi.org/10.1787/9789264040847-en.

Oxford Economics. (2010). *The Size and Health of the UK Space Industry a Report for the UK Space Agency.* London.

Oxford Economics. (2012). *The Size and Health of the UK Space Industry.* London.

Petroni, G., Verbano, C., Bigliardi, B., & Galati, F. (2013). Strategies and Determinants for Successful Space Technology Transfer. *Space Policy, 29*, 251–257. https://doi.org/10.1016/j.spacepol.2013.06.010.

Salter, A. J., & Martin, B. R. (2001). The Economic Benefits of Publicly Funded Basic Research: A Critical Review. *Research Policy, 30*, 509–532. https://doi.org/10.1016/S0048-7333(00)00091-3.

Satellite Applications Catapult. (2014). *Satellites: The Big Picture*. Harwell.

Satellite Applications Catapult. (2019). Scottish Space Incubation Programme [WWW Document]. https://sa.catapult.org.uk/opportunities/scottish-space-incubation-programme/. Accessed 31 Mar 2019.

Scottish Enterprise. (2016). Aerospace, Defence, Marine and Security: Industrial Strategy for Scotland 2016. Edinburgh: Scottish Enterprise.

Scottish Enterprise. (2019). SMART: SCOTLAND Grant for SMEs [WWW Document]. https://www.scottish-enterprise.com/support-for-businesses/funding-and-grants/growing-your-business/smart-scotland-grant. Accessed 6 May 2019.

Space IGS. (2011). The Space Innovation and Growth Strategy: Main Report.

Space IGS. (2014). Space Growth Action Plan.

Space Network Scotland. (2017). Organisational Support for the Space Sector in Scotland [WWW Document]. https://www.space-network.scot/blog/support-for-the-space-sector.html. Accessed 10 May 2019.

STFC. (2013). Higgs Theory 'Gains' Mass! [WWW Document]. https://www.stfc.ac.uk/2960.aspx

STFC. (2018). Higgs Centre for Innovation. https://www.roe.ac.uk/higgscentre/

Tontine. (2018). Join Tontine's Space UK Incubator Programme [WWW Document]. https://www.tontineglasgow.co.uk/Blogs/ViewBlog/36. Accessed 11 May 2019.

UK Space Agency. (2014a). *Government Response to the UK Space Innovation and Growth Strategy 2014–2030*. Space Growth Action Plan. Swindon: UK Space Agency.

UK Space Agency. (2014b). UKube-1—Case Study [WWW Document]. Gov. UK. https://www.gov.uk/government/case-studies/ukube-1. Accessed 10 May 2019.

UK Space Agency. (2015). UKube-1 Completes Mission [WWW Document]. Gov.UK. https://www.gov.uk/government/news/ukube-1-completes-mission. Accessed 10 May 2019.

UK Space Agency. (2017). New Business Incubators Will Help Space Industry Grow. https://www.gov.uk/government/news/new-business-incubators-will-help-space-industry-grow#:~:text=The%20UK%20Space%20Agency%20has,space%20sector%20across%20the%20UK.&text=The%20University%20of%20Leicester%20will,help%20students%20develop%20entrepreneurial%20ideas.

UK Space Agency. (2019). The Wider Benefits of Space Investments for the UK Economy. https://www.gov.uk/government/news/the-wider-benefits-of-space-investments-for-the-uk-economy#:~:text=Investments%20in%20space%20programmes%20bring,society%2C%20a%20new%20report%20shows.&text=Every%20%C2%A31%20of%20public,benefits%20to%20the%20UK%20economy.

Vass, S. (2013). SE Aims to Help Scots Space Firms Conquer the Final Frontier: Winning Funding. *Herald*.

Venturini, K., & Verbano, C. (2014). A Systematic Review of the Space Technology Transfer Literature: Research Synthesis and Emerging Gaps. *Space Policy, 30*, 98–114. https://doi.org/10.1016/j.spacepol.2014.04.003.

Vidmar, M. (2019). Agile Space Living Lab—The Emergence of a New High-Tech Innovation Paradigm. *Space Policy, 49*, 101324.

Vidmar, M. (2020). New Space and Innovation Policy: Scotland's Emerging "Space Glen". *New Space, 8*, 31–51. https://doi.org/10.1089/space.2019.0032.

Vidmar, M. (2021). Enablers, Equippers, Shapers and Movers: A Typology of Innovation Intermediaries Interventions and the Development of an Emergent Innovation System. *Acta Astronautica, 179*, 280–289.

Vidmar, M., Rosiello, A., Williams, R., Vermeulen, N., & Dines, J. (2020). New Space and Agile Innovation: Understanding Transition to Open Innovation Through Examining Innovation Networks and Moments. *Acta Astronautica, 167*, 122–134.

Willetts, D. (2013). *8 Great Technologies, 2013*. London: Policy Exchange.

CHAPTER 4

Systematising Innovation Intermediaries' Interventions

Abstract This chapter argues that closer examination of interventions, rather than organisational roles, is necessary to address issues with the operationalisation of state-of-the-art insights. It proposes a two-step solution—a new (re-)classification of all available interventions based on comprehensive literature review and then the development of a relational typology on the basis of this classification. In particular, the new approach explains and outlines eight classes of interventions (space, knowledge, equipment, skills, interaction, translation, work and capital), grouped into two categories (resources and activities), four sub-categories (infrastructure, tools, framing and project) and split by two qualifiers (social and physical). Furthermore, a typological scheme is developed linking the intervention classification with the innovation intermediaries' organisational capabilities, proposing four critical contextual factors (close involvement, systemic investment, strong vision/mandate and soft leadership) and a typology of innovation intermediaries' roles (enablers, equippers, shapers and movers) as well as correlating them with the evolution of emergent innovation systems.

Keywords Classification • Typology • Innovation intermediaries' interventions • Innovation system • Roles • Functions

M. Vidmar, *Innovation Intermediaries and (Final) Frontiers of High-tech*, https://doi.org/10.1007/978-3-030-60642-8_4

Taking the literature reviews outlined in Chaps. 1 and 2 as a starting point, this chapter exposes how the dividing lines between key studies and approaches are drawn. This is achieved by analysing the key areas of overlap and distinction amongst seven systemic reviews of innovation intermediation literature (Dalziel 2010; Howells 2006; Kilelu et al. 2011; Kim 2015; Kivimaa 2014; Lukkarinen et al. 2018; Nilsson and Sia-Ljungström 2013) as well as incorporating additional studies. The reasoning behind those dividing lines is established by critical analysis of the studies cited within the reviews, which are then also retrofitted with the newly proposed classification framework, in order to test and validate the model, pending further empirical validation. Finally, using the dividing lines, a proto-typological model of contextual factors for deployment of particular interventions is developed. This is then further correlated to the systemic functions performed by innovation intermediaries, to establish a set of typological roles they play in a high-tech ecosystem.

New Classification of Interventions in Geographically-Bound Sectoral Systems of Innovation

When analysing the reviews of innovation intermediation literature and in particular when contrasting the somewhat one-sided classifications as described in the previous chapter, a key set of dividing lines between the studies has emerged. These key differences were exposed as:

- Dalziel is the only study to include specific references to physical space and equipment provision (Dalziel 2010), though Nilsson and Sia-Ljungström (2013) mention broader "physical infrastructure". This is linked to the broader definition of intermediation and the role of support activities (related to cited studies of substantial infrastructural investment) being included in their analysis as a move "beyond the knowledge brokerage" function.
- This led to an additional review of incubation studies (Hackett and Dilts 2004), which exposed a significant emphasis on infrastructural set-up and related financial investment within that segment of the literature, which is otherwise not present. This was further linked to the analysis of political mandate and neutrality, as seen in Kivimaa

(2014) and Klerkx and Leeuwis (2008), related to sectoral emergence/transitioning and stabilisation/maturity.
- Lukkarinen et al. (2018) are the only ones exclusively focusing on soft/relational interventions, though most of the studies are heavily concentrated around brokerage function of intermediaries (Howells 2006; Kim 2015). Such concentration is exposing the interest as well as a contextual focus for these types of interventions. In particular, many studies cited describe lower levels of investment, yet more specific targeted outcomes. These interventions are predominately run by public bodies or trade organisations.
- Many studies allude to direct work done in the innovation process and/or its management (Kim 2015); some also note the deployment of soft capital (Kilelu et al. 2011; Lukkarinen et al. 2018). Examining cited sources shows that these more hands-on types of interventions seem related to early stages of sectoral development (Kivimaa 2014).
- Additional studies reinforce the point above, as there is a significant concentration of studies depicting high level of intermediaries' involvement in early stages of sectoral developments (Agogué et al. 2013; Antikaninen et al. 2009; Katzy et al. 2013), which are missing from those analyses of more systemic activities (Boon et al. 2011; Vonortas 2002) in more mature sectors.

From the above observations, the following three key dividing lines were established between:

- High levels of investment in resources versus active enactment of a strong vision/political mandate: the larger the amount of investment, the more the intermediaries have to be careful to appear neutral as to the vision for the sector and vice versa.
- Specific and targeted hands-on involvement in supporting business or product development versus bigger (more hands-off) systemic support: there is also a significant correlation tentatively noted between these two types of engagement and sector's growth and maturity.
- Interventions which are inherently physical, that is provision of space and equipment, holding meetings, doing work versus those which are social in character, that is development of knowledge and skills, translation of interests, deployment of capital: though it is often the

case that the "physical" interventions are pre-cursors or enablers of the "social" ones.

Building on these observations, the available interventions can be classified using a comprehensive classification, presented in the framework below (see Table 4.1), which is devised to include most available interventions, as analysed in a detailed review of academic literature discussed previously. A detailed analysis of the classification units is presented in the next section.

The classification was constructed using two overarching categories of interventions, resources provision and deployment of activities, as related to the varying focus of interventions from more broad and systemic (such as investments in resources) to more targeted and specific (such as direct activities to shape a particular vision for development). This was derived from the first dividing line finding listed above and seen by a clear direction in some parts of intermediation literature (Howells 2006; Kilelu et al. 2011; Kivimaa 2014; Lukkarinen et al. 2018), which focused predominantly on active engagement with the sector, but somewhat neglected resources provision analysis. It also echoes to a degree the "proactive, reactive, and passive approaches" to intermediation identified by Lichtenthaler (2013).

These categories are then split into subcategories of infrastructure, tools, framing and project, with dividing those with more hands-on types of interventions (such as engaging in projects and developing infrastructure) to those delivered in more hands-off roles (such as sector framing and providing tools for innovation). This is related to the second dividing line established above, specifically noted in the examination of additional sources beyond the seven key literature reviews. On the subcategories level, the classification is further split by intervention qualifiers of being either more "physical" or more "social" in character (first finding). These overarching qualifiers enable the intermediaries to distinguish between deployment of "hard" and "soft" assets, such as buildings and equipment on the one hand, and social capital and thought leadership on the other.

Detailed Analysis of Intervention's Classifications

Taking each of the categories and classes in turn, this section outlines the key analytical work behind framing the resulting classification out of understanding each of the literature's dividing lines, looking beyond the

Table 4.1 Comprehensive classification of intermediaries' interventions based on literature analysis

	Resources *provision of infrastructure and tools for the use of innovation stakeholders*		*Activities* *active engagement in defining and developing future innovation products*	
	Infrastructure *provision of system-level resources*	*Tools* *provision of specific deployable resources*	*Framing* *activities deployed to facilitate wider system development*	*Project* *specific innovation projects to interlink stakeholders and further specific innovation pathways*
Physical	***Space*** Networked provision of physical space for use by stakeholders, i.e. *hireable offices at the intermediary-run facilities; hireable rooms for events*	***Equipment*** Provision of specialist or otherwise inaccessible tools and devices, i.e. *hireable facilities; development of new R&D and qualification environments*	***Interaction*** Active development of opportunities for engagement of stakeholders, i.e. *organisation of, and attendance at, conferences; events; workshop; fora*	***Work*** Active engagement with innovation projects and investment of staff effort, i.e. *work on R&D and commercialisation projects; innovation process management*
Social	***Knowledge*** Systemic provision knowledge (IP) for deployment in innovation processes, i.e. *IP/ knowledge generation and distribution; knowledge mapping and database*	***Skills*** Provision of expertise, advice and workforce, i.e. *hireable expertise; formal training; informal experiences; outreach amongst potential recruits*	***Translation*** Active brokerage between stakeholders and identifying development trends, i.e. *involvement in, and leadership of, the development of policy (reports), standards; sector promotion to stakeholders, other sectors and the wider public*	***Capital*** Active deployment of resources (financial or otherwise) to an innovation project, i.e. *mobilising soft and hard capital for R&D and commercialisation projects*

Note: Categories are split into subcategories and subcategories are further split by qualifiers as described in more detail in the next section.

discussed systemic reviews and into their source material. The resulting analysis is also exposing additional depth to the modalities of delivering the different classes of interventions, suggesting the categories and qualifiers emerging from the dividing lines can be understood in the context of key parameters for operational deployment. In particular, the categorisation and qualification of the various available classes of interventions correspond to the stage of the development of the sector and individual actors as well as demonstrate their dependency on levels of investment and involvement, the strength of vision/mandate and soft leadership embedded in the intermediaries' programmes, which will be outlined in more detail in the next section.

Resources

The resources category is the overarching descriptor for the provision of physical and social infrastructure, such as physical spaces, knowledge/intellectual property (IP), equipment and skills, as needed by the actors in the innovation system. These are often related to significant financial investment and conversely not to a strong vision for the specific technology development focus, in particular, if the funding is from public sources (Hinloopen 2004; Klerkx and Leeuwis 2008). They are divided into two sub-categories, infrastructure and tools, to account for the intensity of hands-on involvement, which is more significant when infrastructure is being developed and deployed, than when tools are provided.

Infrastructure

The systemic provision of infrastructure, such as innovation-supporting physical and social environment/space, is seen as a critical targeted intervention aimed at providing broad-based resources for enterprise formation and development. These resources are most often provided at scale and hence require significant upfront investment (Hackett and Dilts 2004), as well as an extensive close-up management effort to ensure smooth running and development (Kivimaa 2014).

Space

Physical infrastructure in the broadest sense denotes all elements of the built environment needed for hosting business. The most common example is the provision of office space and other facilities, such as internet access (Markides and Anderson 2006). This is often done via the establishment of incubation facilities for start-ups and spin-outs/-offs (Hackett and Dilts 2004) or managed shared office rentals for larger firms (Phan et al. 2005). These resources often include, as vital features, (shared) meeting rooms, social spaces and a bespoke postal address.

Review studies	*Intermediaries' interventions (and reference studies)*
Dalziel (2010)	Physical space (Löfsten and Lindelöf 2002; Phan et al. 2005)
Nilsson and Sia-Ljungström (2013)	System infrastructure creation
	Incubation (Hackett and Dilts 2004)

Knowledge

Knowledge is understood as an enabling factor for innovative enterprise and interventions of this type are targeted at providing or increasing access to knowledge and information, in order to create successful businesses (Abbate et al. 2013; Agogué et al. 2013; Klerkx and Leeuwis 2008). Common examples of specific interventions are the creation and dissemination of knowledge and knowledge management (IP protection support, networking, etc.).

Review studies	*Intermediaries' interventions (and reference studies)*
Howells (2006)	Knowledge processing, generation and combination
Dalziel (2010)	Helping to combine the knowledge or experience of two or more partners, brokering and standards development (Bessant and Rush 1995; Grindley et al. 1994; Howells 2006)
	Intellectual property management and other related activities (Markman et al. 2005; Phan et al. 2005; Siegel et al. 2003)
	Transferring specialised knowledge (Bessant and Rush 1995)
Kivimaa (2014)	Knowledge gathering, processing, generation and combination
	Communication and dissemination of knowledge
Lukkarinen et al. (2018)	Knowledge development and diffusion
Kilelu et al. (2011)	Knowledge brokering
Kim (2015)	Knowledge generation and combination/configuration
	Providing facilities and other knowledge infrastructures
Nilsson and Sia-Ljungström (2013)	Knowledge development and diffusion

(*continued*)

(continued)

Review studies	*Intermediaries' interventions (and reference studies)*
/	Architect of collective exploration (Agogué et al. 2013) Establishing institutional infrastructure (Hargreaves et al. 2012) Bringing in users' knowledge, understanding and opinions to the living lab; integrating heterogeneous knowledge, development ideas, technologies or outputs of different living lab actors into a functional entity (Nyström et al. 2014)

Tools

In contrast to infrastructural provision, the interventions in the "tools" category can be provided with a less significant commitment to the specific users from the innovation intermediaries (Kivimaa 2014). They can be deployed in a much more mobile manner and can reach a far larger number of target recipients. However, through the selection of the equipment and skills provided, the intermediaries can exert a certain degree of influence over the dominant innovation trajectories within the system they serve.

Equipment

Provision of specialist equipment is enabling early-stage firms to innovate and demonstrate the soundness of their innovations (Grindley et al. 1994; Howells 2006; McEvily and Zaheer 1999). This is particularly pertinent in the high-tech sectors, with the need for expensive development tools and high levels of quality assurance (QA). As such, intermediaries can support both NPD and QA processes by providing such equipment which are often prohibitively expensive and of limited return for value for smaller firms. Examples include rentable laboratory space and equipment, qualification equipment or services or software or hardware packages.

Review studies	*Intermediaries' interventions (and reference studies)*
Howells (2006)	Testing, validation (and training)
Dalziel (2010)	Access to expertise and equipment (Mian 1996)
	Possessing resources (Heikkinen et al. 2007) Offering resources for the use of the network; testing innovation in (customers') real-life environments (Nyström et al. 2014)

Skills

In the process of NPD a variety of skills are called for, which are often not all available within a small development team of an SME. Hence, contracted consultative support is required, which is often provided by, or made available through, intermediary organisations. In particular, intermediaries often support skills matching through formal and informal directories and linkages and offer their own skills to companies, particularly in non-product-specific areas such as business development (Mian 1996; Vonortas 2002).

Review studies	*Intermediaries' interventions (and reference studies)*
Howells (2006)	(Testing, validation) and training
Dalziel (2010)	Training activities (McEvily and Zaheer 1999; Mian 1996)
	Advice related to sales and marketing activities (Bessant and Rush 1995)
	Diffusing information and best practice techniques (Grindley et al. 1994)
Kivimaa (2014)	Identification and management of human resource needs (skills)
	Education and training
	Provision of advice and support
	Creating conditions for learning by doing and using
Kilelu et al. (2011)	Capacity building
Kim (2015)	Building new routines and skills through interaction (feedback mechanism)
	Providing access to human resources
	Effectively managing the firm and training employees (Vonortas 2002)
	Aggregating lessons learned (Hargreaves et al. 2012)

Activities

In the activities category fall all those interventions which are predominantly centred around intermediaries pro-actively trying to shape the direction of the economic area they are engaging with, in particular, organising and leading interaction amongst the players, translating interests across different stakeholders, deploying capital to specific projects and carrying out work within the innovation process. They are further split by two subcategories, framing and project, which similarly to resources category above denote the level of involvement by an intermediary, from intense engagement (seen in project-type interventions, often related to emerging sectors) to more hands-off systemic work (in framing-type interventions).

Framing
Framing activities group together interventions which relate to a more systemic leadership role in facilitating interaction and proposing specific visions for future innovation development. This is also vital for wider value chain development, both within a particular sector as well as along its supply chains. They are, hence, linked to stronger intermediation mandates and depend on the deployment of the intermediaries' soft power, extensively analysed in the literature through the concept of brokerage (Howells 2006; Klewitz et al. 2013).

Interaction
A key enabling activity assisting the development of an innovation-rich environment is inter- and intra-sectoral networking (Kilelu et al. 2011; Kivimaa 2014). These interactions take place in meetings, events or through either formal or informal processes of matching, pairing and exchange of ideas. Specifically, intermediaries are often involved in the organisation and/or delivery of conferences, symposia, industry meetings, social events and so on. Through digital communication and social media, some of this interaction is now often facilitated digitally/online (Randhawa et al. 2017).

Review studies	*Intermediaries' interventions (and reference studies)*
Howells (2006)	Gatekeeping and brokering
Kivimaa (2014)	Creation and facilitation of new networks Gatekeeping and brokering
Kilelu et al. (2011)	Network brokering
Kim (2015)	Facilitating interpersonal communications and relationships Bridging links and aligning actors Building trust

(*continued*)

(continued)

Review studies	*Intermediaries' interventions (and reference studies)*
	Network building (Boon et al. 2011) Matchmaking and innovation process design (Katzy et al. 2013) Network brokerage (Klewitz et al. 2013) Support establishment of business enterprise at R&D institutions (Mgumia et al. 2015) Coordinating a group of participants; forwarding and disseminating information in the living lab network (Nyström et al. 2014)

Translation

An important role some innovation intermediaries play is centred on activities aimed at the development of the sector's landscape or framework and brand (Human and Provan 2000; Sapsed et al. 2007). This is in particular related to the promotion of the sector to various internal and external stakeholders, scoping and surveying the state of the actors within the targeted industry, establishment and monitoring of standards and harmonisations, and production of literature and other materials to describe, analyse and promote specific or general innovation opportunities and/or outcomes.

Review studies	*Intermediaries' interventions (and reference studies)*
Howells (2006)	Foresight and diagnosis Scanning and information processing Accreditation and standards Regulation and arbitration Assessment and evaluation
Dalziel (2010)	Standards development and support for systems development (Fuchs 2009; Grindley et al. 1994) Helping users articulate innovation needs (Bessant and Rush 1995) Cluster promotion (Sapsed et al. 2007) Industry promotion (Human and Provan 2000)
Kivimaa (2014)	Articulation of needs, expectations and requirements Advancement of sustainability aims Strategy development Configuring and aligning interests Technology assessment and evaluation Arbitration based on neutrality and trust Policy implementation Accreditation and standard-setting

(*continued*)

(continued)

Review studies	*Intermediaries' interventions (and reference studies)*
Lukkarinen et al. (2018)	Influence on the direction of the search Market formation Legitimation Development of positive externalities
Kilelu et al. (2011)	Institution building Demand articulation
Kim (2015)	Demand articulation Customising knowledge to a specific context Stimulating interaction and enhancing mutual adaptation
Nilsson and Sia-Ljungström (2013)	Guidance of search Market identification and formation Legitimation Locating and approaching the customer, developing relationships of trust, accessing finance (Vonortas 2002) "Management of expectations"; "Urging for action"; "Stay on Track"; "Following others"; "Active case building"; "Administrative consultation"; "Knee-jerk reaction"; "Testing the waters"; "Reflection"; "Unfinished business" (Boon et al. 2011) Demand articulation (Klerkx and Leeuwis 2008) Framing the action and brokering and managing partnerships (Hargreaves et al. 2012) Demonstrate the actual and latent potential of the new technologies (Mgumia et al. 2015) Acting as the initiator; deciding on potential actors; influencing actors' decision-making processes; distributing information externally; promoting its products, services and expertise (Heikkinen et al. 2007) Guiding and supporting the network's activities and continuation; tries to establish trust in the network to boost collaboration to further the living Lab's goals; establishing and promoting the emergence of close relationships between various participants in the living lab (Nyström et al. 2014)

Project

Project-based interventions relate to the specific deployment of activities, which utilise innovation intermediaries' capabilities and resources to further a specific targeted innovation journey (Katzy et al. 2013; Kilelu et al. 2011). As such, this "winner picking" approach is related to both a very hands-on involvement, as well as a strong intermediation mandate, since significant gains can be made by the participating actors (Klerkx and Leeuwis 2008).

Work

Hands-on involvement in project management or delivery is a type of intervention which is predominantly deployed in early-stage companies or new joint venture enterprises, where active participation of an intermediary allows for specific NPD work or harmonisation of interests of several actors (Kivimaa 2014; Klerkx et al. 2015; Mazzoleni and Nelson 2007). These can be formal or informal engagements, crucially with a specific targeted outcome and often anticipated impacts or added value beyond the scope of the project itself.

Review studies	*Intermediaries' interventions (and reference studies)*
Howells (2006)	Intellectual property: protecting the results
Dalziel (2010)	Adapting technologies for alternate applications (Bessant and Rush 1995; Mazzoleni and Nelson 2007)
	Testing and validation of new technologies and equipment (Grindley et al. 1994; McEvily and Zaheer 1999)
Kivimaa (2014)	Acceleration of the application and commercialisation of new technologies
	Prototyping and piloting
	(Long-term) project design, management and evaluation
	Creating new jobs
Lukkarinen et al. (2018)	Entrepreneurial experimentation
Kilelu et al. (2011)	Innovation process management
Nilsson and Sia-Ljungström (2013)	Entrepreneurship
	Facilitation/creation of synergies
	'Project stimulation' (Boon et al. 2011)
	Management of collaborative projects (Katzy et al. 2013)
	Innovation process management (Klerkx et al. 2015)
	Contributing to the development process; participating in development processes (Heikkinen et al. 2007)
	Collaborating intensively with the other actors in the network to develop new products, services, processes or technologies; co-designing a service, product or process together with the company's R&D team and the other living lab actors (Nyström et al. 2014)

Capital

This sub-category's interventions, linked to more hands-off involvement with specific firms and projects, is the investment of capital, which might be financial, in-kind support or even social capital, such as certification or promotion (Antikaninen et al. 2009). Such investments are often made without specific returns in mind, often though competition or tendering set-up, though some are run on a more commercial basis (Mgumia et al. 2015).

Review studies	*Intermediaries' interventions (and reference studies)*
Howells (2006)	Commercialisation: exploiting the outcomes
Kivimaa (2014)	Managing financial resources—finding potential funding and funding activities Investments in new businesses
Lukkarinen et al. (2018)	Resource mobilisation
Kilelu et al. (2011)	Demand stimulation
Nilsson and Sia-Ljungström (2013)	Resource mobilisation
	Non-monetary stimulus (Antikaninen et al. 2009) Project valuation and portfolio management (Katzy et al. 2013) Setting-up of innovation-specific business enterprises (Mgumia et al. 2015) Input in the form of intangible resources (Heikkinen et al. 2007)

From a Classification to a Typology

As referenced throughout the above analysis, mapping out the presented dividing lines also led to a better understanding of the contextual factors, which are framing the innovation intermediaries' interventions and are the backbone of the new classification. These contextual factors are based on innovation intermediaries:

- Having a close hands-on involvement in the innovation process
- Providing large systemic (financial) investment
- Exercising soft leadership
- Enacting a strong vision/mandate

Though not entirely mutually exclusive, these factors seem to establish overall trends in intermediaries' engagement with the innovation system. In turn, these can be linked to some of the literature fragmentation due to competing emergent roles and functions and their divergent prioritisation of various classes of interventions. It seems the sources of said divergence are related to the rationale in the theory of change behind the corresponding innovation policy and particular operationalisation within the intermediary. In the proposed classification, these four factors span across a multitude of classes and categories, establishing a loose coupling of the innovation intermediaries' positions within any studied sector and the interventions deployed.

The resulting typological framing is best visually represented as a concentric continuum in a four-cornered/diamond scheme (see Fig. 4.1).

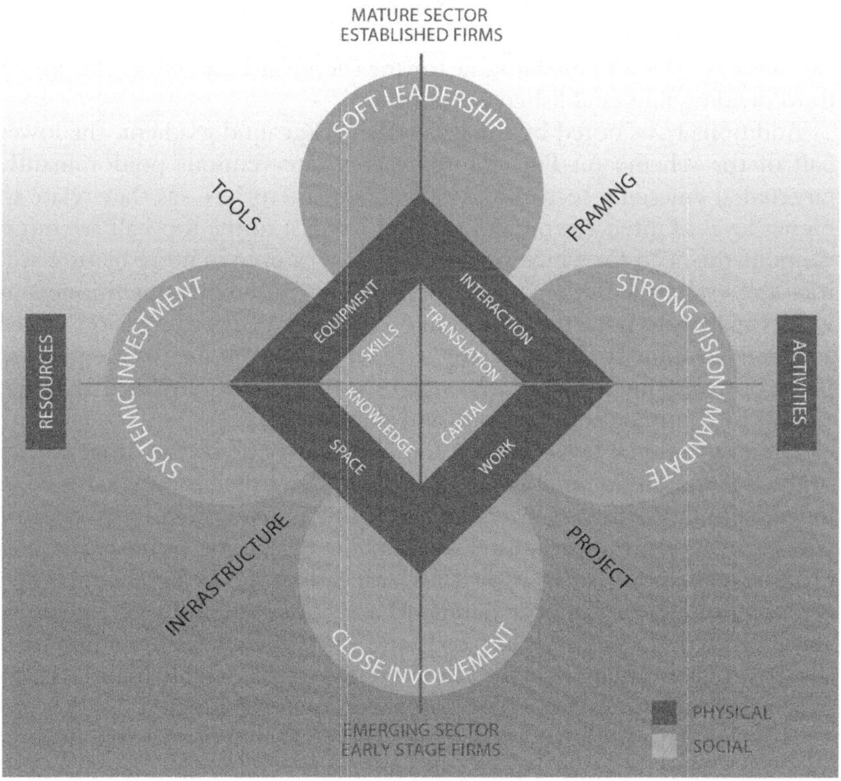

Fig. 4.1 Innovation intermediaries' interventions typology scheme. The central diamond is formed of intermediaries' classification categories, with contextual factors related to the four categories and eight intervention classes. Schematically, the resources versus activities division runs left to right, whilst emergence to maturity development stretched from bottom to the top

The contextual factors (the bubbles in pink) show the type of intermediaries' agenda/mandate/position within the sector as reflected in and shaped by undertaking specific classes of interventions. Thus, the framework schema describes the need for high levels of involvement to deliver direct interventions within and around supporting firms (on the bottom); requirement for significant investment to deliver equipment and physical space and develop provision of new knowledge and training (on the left); the importance of a significant mandate and associated social capital to guide innovation processes (on the right); and a soft leadership approach to facilitating geo-sectoral interaction and translation of interests and definition of needs (on the top). Furthermore, the social types of interventions are deliberately embedded within a wider frame of physical ones, as the latter is often the enabling factor for the former, as referenced in the third dividing line established previously.

Additionally, as noted by the greyscale background gradient, the lower half of the scheme on Fig. 4.1 represents interventions predominantly targeted at emerging sectors and early-stage enterprises—as they relate to higher level of intervention and support—whilst in the top half are interventions the need for which continues to persist even in more mature sectors and established companies. Such view enables both practitioners as well as analysis to trace the evolution on the intermediary provision as well as the development of the sector it is serving, from an early emerging phase of strong involvement, through investment and mutual co-shaping, and on to consolidation, maturity and stabilisation.

On an individual level, tipping the balance to one or the other corner of the typological framing will be related to where the primary focus of an individual intermediary's intervention programme(s) is. In most cases, it will be either on infrastructural investments or specific trendsetting and project work (most usually associated with early stages of an emerging sector/technology) or on more hands-off activities such as providing spaces and incentives for defining of trends and easing key skills and equipment shortages (associated with the development of commercialisation pathways and R&D consolidation of later stages of development).

However, an additional understanding is needed of the way the deployment of (classes of) interventions and their contextual factors are linked to a typology of intermediaries' organisational roles and their set-up. Examining the literature, Kilelu et al. define six functions to innovation intermediaries' interventions as "demand articulation/stimulation, network brokering, knowledge brokering, innovation process management, capacity building and institutional building" (Kilelu et al. 2011, p. 13) and Klerkx and Leeuwis (2008) pose innovation intermediaries as solving five challenges: demand articulation, developing resources and competencies, dealing with market failures, financing and overcoming system failures.

Hence, integrating these functional assessments of intermediaries' roles within an ecosystem with the four contextual factors a new typological model is proposed. In addition to the theoretical framing, this also reflects the aims of the analysed empirical examples from previous chapter, as will be further examined in Chap. 5. Overall, it is proposed that taking into account the contextual deployment of innovation intermediaries' interventions, they converge at having four main types of roles (as per Vidmar (2021)):

- To remove barriers for innovation by providing resources and action to address bottlenecks and challenges, with typical core intervention classes being Skills Resources and Capital Activities. These are usually linked to close involvement in the day-to-day support of innovators and can be seen as the type of interventions *enabling the ecosystem.*
- To proactively create conditions encouraging innovation, with stimulus, promotion and investment with deploying Space and Equipment Resources. These interventions normally require significant systemic investment, with a specific intention to develop the capacity for *equipping the players.*
- To create a purchase in the innovation, especially by assisting in the development of markets, often external to the sector, through Interaction and Translation Activities. These interventions are usually predicated on soft leadership capacity within intermediaries and are intended to help *shaping the common vision.*
- To enact a particular vision for the future of the activity in a sector through delivering Work Activities and deploying Knowledge Resources. In order for innovation intermediaries to develop such interventions, they require a strong mandate with significant political (often financial) and social capital and are designed to be *moving the development.*

These roles also correspond to some of the existing summative organisation typologies studied earlier. In particular, as shown in Table 4.2, this

Table 4.2 Alignment of lead contextual factors, typology of intermediaries' roles and selected past studies

The core of typological model		*Correspondence to past studies*		
Lead contextual factors	*Typology of intermediaries' roles*	*Kilelu* et al. (2011)	*Colombo, Dell'Era, and Frattini* (2015)	*Kim* (2015)
Close involvement	Enabling the ecosystem	Input access-focused	Broker	Knowledge enabling
Systemic investment	Equipping the players	Technology brokers	Connector	Managing interfaces
Soft leadership	Shaping the common vision	Systemic brokers	Mediator	Facilitating relations
Strong vision/ mandate	Moving the development	Enterprise development support	Collector	Facilitating learning

typology aligns with Kilelu et al. (2011), Colombo, Dell'Era, and Frattini (2015) and Kim (2015), each putting forward a four-partite breakdown of the (eco)systemic roles played by intermediary organisations. For instance, Kilelu et al. (2011) highlight the distinction between operating on a systemic level and within specific domains (in firms or specific technology area). In addition, Colombo, Dell'Era, and Frattini (2015) focus on the diversification of interventions between interventions addressing sources of knowledge, experience and competences, relationships and solutions. Going even further, Kim (2015) provides even more detail, noting the difference in intermediaries supporting the development of core knowledge and technology, providing facilities and other resources, brokering links between actors and stimulating interaction and mutual adaptation.

In addition, it is important to note that the four roles cover a very wide range of actual deployment configurations of the classes of interventions. They are also not mutually exclusive and intermediaries, in particular ones with a larger mandate and bigger organisational capacity, can fulfil multiple ones. In order to explore and explain further the manifestation of these roles, a set of real-life examples and empirical data may be called upon. Past studies show that such understanding is very context-specific (Klerkx et al. 2015; Martin and Scott 2000), depending on the sector, the local environment and so on.

In summary, the proposed novel classification of innovation intermediaries' interventions can be used as a critical way to systematise and structure the provision of resources and deployment of activities these organisations put forward in support of an emerging high-tech ecosystem. However, further analysis of the deployment of the intervention classes is needed, to deepen the link between the contextual factors presented, the typology of intermediaries' roles and the intentions of the interventions deployed. As will be explored in next chapter, such analysis also frames the innovation intermediaries' organisational structure and their aims in a studied Geographically-Bound Sectoral System of Innovation.

Bibliography

Abbate, T., Coppolino, R., & Schiavone, F. (2013). Linking Entities in Knowledge Transfer: The Innovation Intermediaries. *Journal of the Knowledge Economy, 4*, 233–243. https://doi.org/10.1007/s13132-013-0156-5.

Agogué, M., Ystrom, A., & Le Masson, P. (2013). Rethinking the Role of Intermediaries as an Architect of Collective Exploration and Creation of Knowledge in Open Innovation. *International Journal of Innovation Management, 17*, 1350007. https://doi.org/10.1142/S1363919613500072.

Antikaninen, M., Mäkipää, M., & Ahonen, M. (2009). Motivating and Supporting Collaboration in Open Innovation. *Technology Management, 13*, 24.

Bessant, J., & Rush, H. (1995). Building Bridges for Innovation: The Role of Consultancies in Technology Transfer. *Research Policy, 24*, 97–114. https://doi.org/10.1016/0048-7333(93)00751-E.

Boon, W. P., Moors, E. H., Kuhlmann, S., & Smits, R. E. (2011). Demand Articulation in Emerging Technologies: Intermediary User Organisations as Co-Producers? *Research Policy, 40*, 242–252.

Colombo, M. G., Dell'Era, C., & Frattini, F. (2015). Contribution of Innovation Intermediaries to NPD Process. *R&D Management, 45*, 126–146.

Dalziel, M. (2010). Why Do Innovation Intermediaries Exist? In *Druid 2010: Opening Up Innovation: Strategy, Organization and Technology* (p. 23). London: Imperial College London Business School.

Fuchs, E. (2009). *The Role of DARPA in Seeding and Encourage New Technology Trajectories.* Sloan Industry Studies Working Papers 2001–2009.

Grindley, P., Mowery, D. C., & Silverman, B. (1994). SEMATECH and Collaborative Research: Lessons in the Design of High-Technology Consortia. *Journal of Policy Analysis and Management, 13*, 723. https://doi.org/10.2307/3325495.

Hackett, S. M., & Dilts, D. M. (2004). A Systematic Review of Business Incubation Research. *The Journal of Technology Transfer, 29*, 55–82. https://doi.org/10.1023/B:JOTT.0000011181.11952.0f.

Hargreaves, T., Hielscher, S., Seyfang, G., & Smith, A. (2012). Exploring the Roles of Intermediaries in UK Community Energy: Grassroots Innovations and Niche Development. *Science, Society & Sustainability, 23*, 1–26.

Heikkinen, M. T., Mainela, T., Still, J., & Tähtinen, J. (2007). Roles for Managing in Mobile Service Development Nets. *Industrial Marketing Management, 36*, 909–925. https://doi.org/10.1016/j.indmarman.2007.05.014.

Hinloopen, J. (2004). The Market for Knowledge Brokers. *Small Business Economics, 22*, 407–415. https://doi.org/10.1023/B:SBEJ.0000022210.10016.28.

Howells, J. (2006). Intermediation and the Role of Intermediaries in Innovation. *Research Policy, 35*, 715–728. https://doi.org/10.1016/j.respol.2006.03.005.

Human, S. E., & Provan, K. G. (2000). Legitimacy Building in the Evolution of Small-Firm Multilateral Networks: A Comparative Study of Success and Demise. *Administrative Science Quarterly, 45*, 327. https://doi.org/10.2307/2667074.

Katzy, B., Turgut, E., Holzmann, T., & Sailer, K. (2013). Innovation Intermediaries: A Process View on Open Innovation Coordination. *Technology Analysis & Strategic Management, 25*, 295–309. https://doi.org/10.1080/09537325.2013.764982.

Kilelu, C. W., Klerkx, L., Leeuwis, C., & Hall, A. (2011). Beyond Knowledge Brokering: An Exploratory Study on Innovation Intermediaries in an Evolving Smallholder Agricultural System in Kenya. *Knowledge Management for Development Journal, 7*, 84–108. https://doi.org/10.1080/19474199.2011.593859.

Kim, E. S. (2015). *Facilitating Innovation in SMEs: The Case of Public Intermediaries in South Korea* [Doctoral Thesis]. Edinburgh: The University of Edinburgh.

Kivimaa, P. (2014). Government-Affiliated Intermediary Organisations as Actors in System-Level Transitions. *Research Policy, 43*, 1370–1380. https://doi.org/10.1016/j.respol.2014.02.007.

Klerkx, L., & Leeuwis, C. (2008). Matching Demand and Supply in the Agricultural Knowledge Infrastructure: Experiences with Innovation Intermediaries. *Food Policy, 33*, 260–276. https://doi.org/10.1016/J.FOODPOL.2007.10.001.

Klerkx, L., Álvarez, R., & Campusano, R. (2015). The Emergence and Functioning of Innovation Intermediaries in Maturing Innovation Systems: The Case of Chile. *Innovation and Development, 5*, 73–91. https://doi.org/10.1080/2157930X.2014.921268.

Klewitz, J., Zeyen, A., & Hansen, E. G. (2013). Intermediaries Driving Eco-Innovation in SMEs: A Qualitative Investigation. *European Journal of Innovation Management, 15*, 442–467. https://doi.org/10.1108/14601061211272376.

Lichtenthaler. (2013). Markets for Technology: The Definition. *Journal of Product Innovation Management, 30*, 1–9.

Löfsten, H., & Lindelöf, P. (2002). Science Parks and the Growth of New Technology-Based Firms—Academic-Industry Links, Innovation and Markets. *Research Policy, 31*, 859–876. https://doi.org/10.1016/S0048-7333(01)00153-6.

Lukkarinen, J., Berg, A., Salo, M., Tainio, P., Alhola, K., & Antikainen, R. (2018). An Intermediary Approach to Technological Innovation Systems (TIS)—The Case of the Cleantech Sector in Finland. In *Environmental Innovation and Societal Transitions* (pp. 136–146). https://doi.org/10.1016/j.eist.2017.04.003.

Markides, C. C., & Anderson, J. (2006). Creativity Is Not Enough: ICT-Enabled Strategic Innovation. *European Journal of Innovation Management, 9*, 129–148. https://doi.org/10.1108/14601060610663532.

Markman, G. D., Phan, P. H., Balkin, D. B., & Gianiodis, P. T. (2005). Entrepreneurship and University-Based Technology Transfer. *Journal of Business Venturing, 20*, 241–263. https://doi.org/10.1016/j.jbusvent.2003.12.003.

Martin, S., & Scott, J. T. J. T. (2000). The Nature of Innovation Market Failure and the Design of Public Support for Private Innovation. *Research Policy, 29*, 437–447. https://doi.org/10.1016/S0048-7333(99)00084-0.

Mazzoleni, R., & Nelson, R. R. (2007). Public Research Institutions and Economic Catch-Up. *Research Policy, 36*, 1512–1528. https://doi.org/10.1016/j.respol.2007.06.007.

McEvily, B., & Zaheer, A. (1999). Bridging Ties: A Source of Firm Heterogeneity in Competitive Capabilities. *Strategic Management Journal, 20*, 1133–1156. https://doi.org/10.1002/(SICI)1097-0266(199912)20:12<1133::AID-SMJ74>3.0.CO;2-7.

Mgumia, A. H., Mattee, A. Z., & Kundi, B. A. T. (2015). Contribution of Innovation Intermediaries in Agricultural Innovation: The Case of Agricultural R&D in Tanzania. *African Journal of Science, Technology, Innovation and Development, 7*, 151–160. https://doi.org/10.1080/20421338.2015.1023644.

Mian, S. (1996). Assessing Value-Added Contributions of University Technology Business Incubators to. Tenant Firms'. *Research Policy, 25*, 325–335.

Nilsson, M., & Sia-Ljungström, C. (2013, February 18–23). The Role of Innovation Intermediaries in Innovation Systems. In *2013 International European Forum* (pp. 161–180). Innsbruck/Igls: International European Forum on System Dynamics and Innovation in Food Networks.

Nyström, A. G., Leminen, S., Westerlund, M., & Kortelainen, M. (2014). Actor Roles and Role Patterns Influencing Innovation in Living Labs. *Industrial Marketing Management, 43*, 483–495. https://doi.org/10.1016/j.indmarman.2013.12.016.

Phan, P. H., Siegel, D. S., & Wright, M. (2005). Science Parks and Incubators: Observations, Synthesis and Future Research. *Journal of Business Venturing, 20*, 165–182. https://doi.org/10.1016/j.jbusvent.2003.12.001.

Randhawa, K., Josserand, E., Schweitzer, J., & Logue, D. (2017). Knowledge Collaboration Between Organizations and Online Communities: The Role of Open Innovation Intermediaries. *Journal of Knowledge Management, 21*, 1293–1318. https://doi.org/10.1108/JKM-09-2016-0423.

Sapsed, J., Grantham, A., & De Fillippi, R. (2007). A Bridge Over Troubled Waters: Bridging Organizations and Entrepreneurial Opportunities in Emerging Sectors. *Research Policy, 36*, 1314.

Siegel, D. S., Waldman, D., & Link, A. (2003). Assessing the Impact of Organizational Practices on the Relative Productivity of University Technology Transfer Offices: An Exploratory Study. *Research Policy, 32*, 27–48. https://doi.org/10.1016/S0048-7333(01)00196-2.

Vidmar, M. (2021). Enablers, Equippers, Shapers and Movers: A typology of innovation intermediaries interventions and the development of an emergent innovation system. *Acta Astronautica, 179*, 280–289.

Vonortas, N. S. (2002). Building Competitive Firms: Technology Policy Initiatives in Latin America. *Technology in Society, 24*, 433–459. https://doi.org/10.1016/S0160-791X(02)00034-9.

CHAPTER 5

New Innovation Intermediation Model for New Space

Abstract This chapter re-examines the case of innovation intermediaries in the emerging New Space sector in peripheral countries. It starts with two comparative studies of two innovation intermediaries, one in Scotland and one in Slovenia, with reference to the innovation policy context. Starting from a comparable investment and relatively similar environment, these two organisations developed a very different set of interventions, noting their perspective on the emergent innovation system, as well as wider political context related to their set-up, in the particular smart specialisation. This is followed by a summative analysis of the provisions and the evolution of the Scottish innovation intermediation landscape deploying the newly proposed classification, contextual factors and typology.

Keywords New Space sector • Scotland • Slovenia • Innovation policy • Smart specialisation strategy • Heuristic use of model

Expanding the definition of innovation intermediaries and developing a new classification and typology of their interventions, as proposed in the previous chapters, still leave open the question of operational deployment. In particular, a more detailed understanding of the developmental links between the ecosystem roles, contextual factors, intervention classes and the external environment is needed to establish comprehensive and coherent logic for intervention development. This also requires a closer

M. Vidmar, *Innovation Intermediaries and (Final) Frontiers of High-tech*, https://doi.org/10.1007/978-3-030-60642-8_5

examination of the policymaking and operational deployment decisions, as well as a contextual understanding of geo-sectoral innovation landscape, within a Geographically-Bound Sectoral System of Innovation.

As shown earlier, using the links between the dividing lines in the literature, the contextual factors related to their emergence were derived—that is Close Involvement, Systemic Investment, Soft Leadership and Strong Mandate. These four factors loosely correspond to the structure of intervention classes, paired as Project and Infrastructure, Infrastructure and Tools, Tools and Framing and Framing and Project respectively. The underlying divisions between the four groups and their contexts reflect the tensions between the economic requirements of acquiring and deploying resources and political commitments in proposing and delivering activities. There is also an implied development trajectory running through these groups, mirroring a degree of ecosystem's evolution from emergence to maturity.

Moreover, a typology was established to highlight the (eco)system roles intermediaries undertake within a Geographically-Bound Sectoral System of Innovation (GSSI). These comprise of Enablers (removing barriers and provide resources), Equippers (develop conditions in support of innovation), Shapers (creating alignment and purchase across players) and Movers (engaging in direct support for specific projects and technologies). The four types of roles relate to the outputs of the interventions, which are somewhat conditioned by the contextual factors; however, the details of these relationships require further study.

It is further important to note that the above interventions' objectives are underpinned by contextual processes of organisational learning within intermediaries (Hyysalo and Stewart 2008; Ngwenya and Hagmann 2011) and reflecting the wider innovation system development (Kivimaa 2014). Hence this model could also be used as a tool in understanding the organisational set-up and development of individual intermediaries. Of particular interest would be comparing organisational and systemic development across different sectors within the same socio-economic and political context (i.e. locale, region, state) or between two different geographical contexts. This is also linked to the variety of underlying factors in policymaking (Flanagan et al. 2011).

As before, empirical focus turns to New Space sector, whilst in order to add geographical comparison, the research extends to another peripheral country in terms of existing space industry—Slovenia. The New Space industrial activities started to develop the mid-2000s in both countries (and globally). In Scotland, the sector evolved from a set of entrepreneurial activities and knowledge spill-over from a few leading universities. In contrast to Slovenia, the sector in Scotland only started to attract more substantial policy investment after the entrepreneurial activities were launched (i.e. after 2010), whilst in Slovenia, the innovation intermediation interventions were intended to kick-start the activities (in 2009). Hence, there is a clearly different set of path-dependencies at play in the two countries' policies—leading to diverging classes of interventions, contextual factors and intermediaries' typologies.

Hence, to begin with, a comparative case study looking at international differences in the organisational set-up of intermediaries (Vidmar 2019a) validates the general usability of the proposed model. Subsequently, the differentiating aspects of the four innovation intermediaries' roles are discussed by re-examining the set of four case studies presented in Chap. 3. This is contextualised with a piece of empirical research summarising the needs and provisions of the sector, as seen by intermediation practitioners, which demonstrates the classification and typology's analytical power.

From Policy to Practice: Comparisons Between Organisations and Contexts

In order to understand the contextual nature of the innovation intermediation interventions' design and deployment, the use of classification and typology framework in two different contextual environments with common developmental trajectory and similar ambition is proposed. In particular, the study shown here focused on two innovation intermediaries' organisational set-up, which are based within a similar area of development—that is the same sector/technological domain, a similar level of investment, similar position within the innovation policy context and so on—yet in two different geographical, political and socio-economic contexts. This allowed for the identification of those factors which influence the potentially divergent application of classes of interventions.

Hence, in this section, two carefully selected case studies are presented of two innovation intermediaries, both supported by significant direct public investment, in two different yet comparable geopolitical contexts. Specifically, the studied organisations support the development of the New Space sector in geopolitical locales that were previously peripheral in this domain—in Scotland and in Slovenia. The two countries share somewhat similar broad geographical disposition: both are NUTS1 regions[1] of the European Union with a few million inhabitants, of stunning and diverse natural environments, and regarded as tourism, food and drink and only more recently high-tech destinations. However, the two countries have a diverging socio-economic and political context, which led to different prioritisation in government investment in the support for the emerging New Space sector. The differences are related to both the economic and research activities and infrastructure, as well as to the path-dependency of the two countries' innovation policy (Farole et al. 2010).

These were examined further by studying more closely the two flagship innovation intermediation investments in the two countries: the Slovenian centre Space-SI (established in 2009) and the Scottish Higgs Centre for Innovation (established in 2013), the later of which was already presented earlier. Using document analysis and interviews with key staff, as well as longitudinal ethnographic work, a detailed set of contextual factors was established to compare and contrast the establishment and operation of the two organisations and the deployed interventions, as shown in Table 5.1.

The findings show that though both of the organisations deliver support in the research and development (R&D) and business development (BD) domains—the primary focus for Space-SI is R&D and for Higgs Centre for Innovation is BD. This is related to a clear divide that the Slovenian intermediary is predominantly focusing on enacting a vision, whilst the Scottish one is more focused on equipping innovators. Consequently, the Space-SI centre is delivering on project work and developing new knowledge, whilst the Higgs Centre for Innovation is providing physical space and equipment, as well as skills and interaction (classes of interventions). Both intermediaries provide a degree of systemic investment with some close involvement, while the Slovenian Space-SI additionally enacts a strong vision/mandate.

The emerging differences can be understood in the context of the set-up and development of the two organisations. For instance, there is greater ability to enact a vision for the Space-SI, as the investment was developed competitively, through a bidding process via an open call, legitimising the

[1] Following European Union's Nomenclature of Units for Territorial Statistics (NUTS) Level 1 (top-level) regional definition framework (*Regulation (EC) No 1059/2003 of the European Parliament and of the Council of 26 May 2003 on the establishment of a common classification of territorial units for statistics (NUTS)*, 2018).

Table 5.1 Comparison of contextual factors across the two cases, showing how critical differences in policy environment lead to a divergent operational set-up of an intervention (classes) prioritisation

Policy approach / *Contextual factors**	*Niche specialisation*	*Regional advantage*
Policy ethos	Entrepreneurial discovery	Stakeholder-driven policy
Critical elements	Policy process, market, competition	Geography, relatedness, ecosystem
Policy action	Facilitating self-discovery	Removing bottlenecks/ stimulating innovation
Case study	***Space-SI (Slovenia)***	***Higgs Centre for Innovation (Scotland)***
Policy set-up process	Competitive negotiation of interests through open bid	Policy design within government agencies
Level of maturity	Low	Intermediate
Lead stakeholders	Academia + business	Government/NGOs + academia
Lead users	Established firms	Start-ups
Main policy principle	"Capitalise on advantage(s)"	"Neutrality"
Intermediaries' **intervention prototypological driver**	Strong mandate	Systemic investment
Main type of innovation intermediation role	Enacting a vision	Equipping the players
Main support focus	**R&D**	**BD**
Implementation ethos	"Steering development"	"Satisfying demand"
Surrounding network	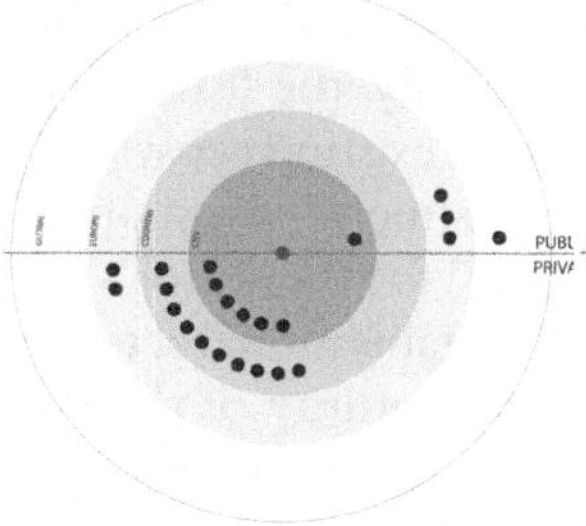	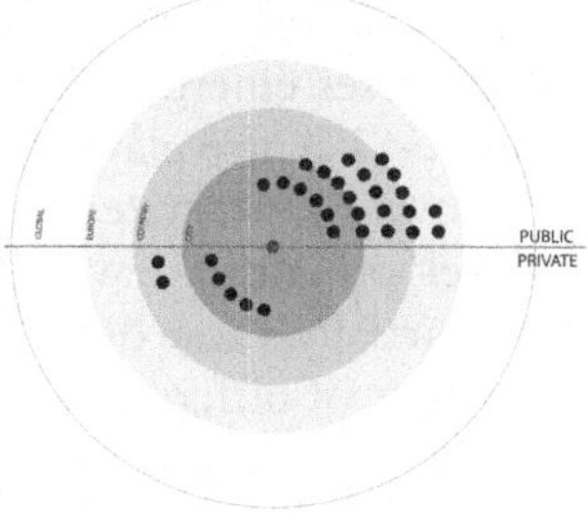

Source: Vidmar (2019a)

*Derived primarily from Boschma (2013) and Asheim (2013)

vision behind the proposed programme. In contrast, the Higgs Centre for Innovation was designed through closed-door governmental policy mechanisms with industry input, making the distribution of interventions a site for open competition as to maintain technological neutrality, that is to avoid perception of the public policymakers prioritising particular products and services (Azar and Sandén 2011; Gross et al. 2010). Specifically, Space-SI was explicitly designed to develop projects leading to applied research solutions in niche areas by integrating diverse actors across the science and business community. While the Higgs Centre for Innovation is tapping into a similar overall policy vision in the UK, the support for New Space sector can be traced back to the Eight Great Technologies white paper (Willetts 2013), its focus is firmly in providing resources for start-ups and early-stage SMEs (Kerry and Danson 2016). As a consequence, the Slovenian centre is steering the sector development by creating innovation supply through project work, while the Scottish one attempting to satisfy the demand for space and equipment resources.

One of the crucial questions in innovation intermediation is who are the users of any given intervention (Hyysalo and Stewart 2008). The primary target users of the Space-SI program are established companies looking for new opportunities and markets, whereas the Higgs Centre for Innovation is more explicitly aiming to support emerging economic actors, that is spin-off and start-up SMEs. This is clearly visible in the innovation network positioning of the two centres—the Slovenian has many more (established) private sector partners, whereas the Scottish one is more engaged with public sector ones, in particular academia, from where many of the new businesses emerge. Consequently, the "strong vision" put forward by the Space-SI centre plays out in an existing ecosystem and the Higgs Centre for Innovation's "systemic investment" is supporting and promoting the development of new "visions" for the sector's economic activities.

Partially, these different organisational set-ups can be understood in the context of different levels of maturity of the emerging New Space sector in the two countries at the time of the intermediaries' establishment. In addition, due to significant set of regulatory constraints the commercialisation efforts of the Space-SI centre are only now emerging (Stare et al. 2014). Conversely, it is equally uncertain what the actual full intervention delivery of Higgs Centre for Innovation will be on the Scottish New Space sector since it has only become operational in 2018.

However, organisational differences within economic development policy can also be explained in societal terms (Farole et al. 2010) by examining policy rationales, objectives and implementation approaches. Here, differences can emerge as a result of the interaction and tension between different levels and aspects of policymaking and its participants (Blair 2002; Flanagan et al. 2011). For example, our case studies point towards a set of significant differences in the political ideology surrounding innovation policy between the two contexts. In the case of Space-SI in Slovenia, the intervention is delivered through significant direct investment in the development of specific projects led by the academia, with commercial applications only as a later-stage/additional outcome (Bucar 2015). In contrast, in the Scottish case of Higgs Centre for Innovation, the objectives of innovation policy and the resulting intermediary organisation(s) are to directly target and involve business interests from the start, with academic research investment being covered (or not) by separate science funding (Edler et al. 2013). This has been identified in a myriad of cases beyond the study presented here, where researchers examined incubation facilities, accelerators and networks (Slovenian universities' technology parks and incubators, UK-wide KTN and Catapult networks, etc.) (Kerry and Danson 2016; Bučar and Rissola 2018).

In addition, there is a significantly diverging definition of scientific impact at play between the two policymaking contexts—focusing on a clear economic benefit in Scotland (and the UK), whilst being more flexible and interpretative in Slovenia. In particular, Scottish and UK policymakers put greater emphasis on efficiency in BD innovation support (Nishimura and Okamuro 2011) than the Slovenian ones. However, this may not always be for the best—as overreliance on BD support may lead to poor R&D investment and subsequent decline in competitive advantage. This has been recognised in Scotland/UK and the scope and scale of R&D funding are currently being addressed through Challenge Funding and place-based City Deals available through the UK's industrial strategy (HM Government 2017). In contrast, Slovenia's lack of support for BD meant that though in many ways with superior in R&D it is losing out to countries like Scotland which capitalise on being first to bring solutions to the market, such as by establishing the Agile Space brand (Vidmar 2019b, 2020).

In fact, these diverging policies have an extended effect on the innovation intermediation landscape in Scotland. Having shown the detailed analysis of the significance of the innovation intermediaries for the emergence of the Scottish New Space sector in Chap. 3, the next section applies the novel model to understand better the evolution of their interventions.

Evolution of Innovation Intermediation Interventions in the Scottish New Space Sector

Going back to the four cases presented in Chap. 3, re-examining these leading interventions illustrates the interconnectedness of the contextual factors, classification qualifiers and groupings and the typological roles of enabling, equipping, shaping and moving the development, which has been derived from the state of the art in the literature.

Overall, as expected, the four case studies show a significant degree of organisational divergence, according to their objectives. Examining the cross-section of the four studied intermediaries' intervention classifications, lead contextual factors and typological characterisation, as shown in Table 5.2, it is clear that the different classes of intervention arise within different contextual factors, leading to the intermediaries serving different (eco)systemic roles. It is further noted that these correlate to diverging organisational set-ups, with public funding and direct project management most intensely present in the emerging phase interventions requiring close involvement and strong vision/mandate, whilst significant investment aligns with more neutral and at arm's length engagement, whilst soft leadership is both at arm's length and with low capital support.

In addition to better understanding the organisational set-up within the developed model of interventions, the needs and provisions within a geo-sectoral context can be examined using the same classification and typological tools. As part of the same study, four typical cases of intermediaries staff were interviewed (Vidmar 2021). Asked about the general needs of a provision of interventions within the Scottish New Space ecosystem, as well as their own organisation's contributions, the following picture of interventions' demand and supply has emerged, as can be seen in Fig. 5.1.

As can be seen, the intervention classes comprising capital, work and interaction have the highest level of provision. This reasonably well matched to greatest needs, which also fall in those classes. Space resources have the lowest provision, reasonably well satisfied. However, using a simple subtraction between needs and provisions, some critical discrepancies between interventions' demand and supply emerge. Largest

Table 5.2 Cross-sectional analysis of the four typical case studies. In part summarised from Vidmar (2021)

Innovation intermediation organisations	*Key intermediation interventions*	*Key characteristics*	*Intervention classification(s)*	*Lead contextual factors*	*Typological classification*	*Organisational set-up*
Scottish Enterprise	SMART: Scotland Awards—*Space Network Scotland (SNS)*	Open regional grants scheme; funding to successful applicants—*Facilitating networking*	Capital Skills—*Interaction*	Close Involvement—*Soft leadership*	Enabling—*Shaping*	Systemic mechanism developed and managed by governmental innovation agency—SNS can be treated as an evolution of the provision, as it is at arm's length and competitively (small) funded
Science and Technology Facilities Council (part of UK Research and Innovation)	Higgs Centre for Innovation	Business incubator programme and innovation facility; funding and access to expertise and equipment, events facilitation	Space Skills Equipment Knowledge Interaction	Systemic investment	Equipping	Large government investment developed and managed by a research facilities organisation

(*continued*)

Table 5.2 (continued)

Innovation intermediation organisations	*Key intermediation interventions*	*Key characteristics*	*Intervention classification(s)*	*Lead contextual factors*	*Typological classification*	*Organisational set-up*
Scottish Centre of Excellence in Satellite Applications (SoXA)	Scottish Space Symposium/ DATA.SPACE conference	Series of events of regional and international reach; facilitating networking and discussions	Interaction Translation	Soft leadership	Shaping	Flagship project affiliated with large national programme developed and managed by a small local team based within a research organisation (small funding)
UK Government/ UK Space Agency	UKube-1	Directly designed project with lead partners; funding and project management	Work Capital Knowledge	Strong vision/ mandate	Moving	Small-scale government investment into a specific project developed by SMEs and managed by a corporate partner

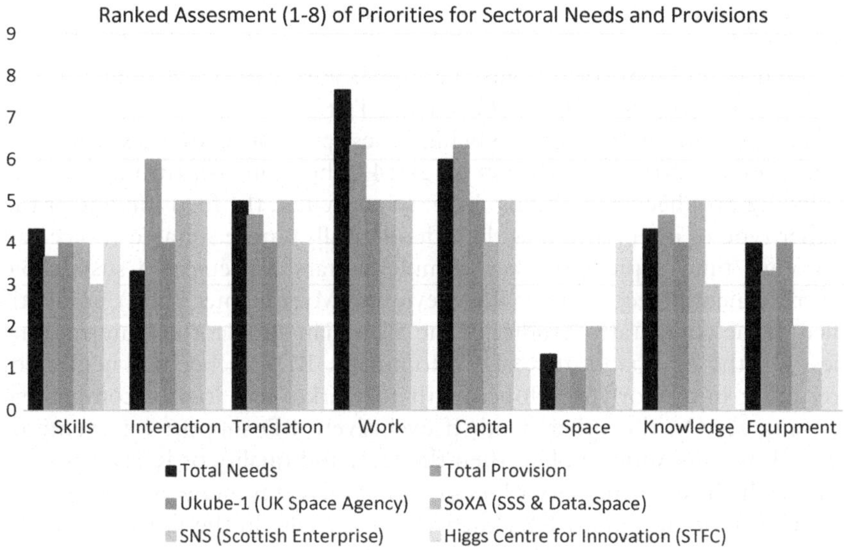

Fig. 5.1 Summative total of needs and provision assessment and intervention focus for Scottish New Space innovation intermediaries, broken down by the classification. (Source: Vidmar 2021)

negative difference (i.e. under-provision) is in the class of work (net difference of -1.3), whilst the most overprovided is interaction (difference of +2.7). There are also negative sums for skills and equipment (-0.7), as well as space and translation (-0.3), though there seems to be a slight overprovision of knowledge and capital (+0.3). This highlights that summatively, there is a strong intermediaries' focus on fulfilling "shaping" roles within the innovation system, with a lack of attention to "moving" innovation.

Such analysis can form a clear basis for a holistic view of the variety of roles intermediaries (can) play in innovation systems. Insight derived this way can help with recognising the importance of organisations previously excluded from the intermediation typologies as well as to detect and address gaps in the provision of interventions. In particular, tools can be developed around heuristic use of the proposed model, both on the level of intervention's classification (resources/activities, physical/social, systemic/direct), the contextual factors (close involvement, systemic investment, soft leadership and strong mandate) as well as the emerging comprehensive typology of roles (enablers, equippers, shapers and movers).

Hence, different socio-political contexts are clearly co-shaping innovation policy (Bennett 2008). Given the fact that institutional obduracy builds a significant momentum behind these path-dependencies (Boschma and Frenken 2011; Valdaliso et al. 2014), they can also turn into a self-fulfilling prophecy-like vicious circle. In particular, the focus on one or the other type of intervention as the (ideologically) more suitable choice can through time deplete the key complementary aspects of a sustainable entrepreneurial (eco)system (Radosevic and Myrzakhmet 2009), as identified in the comparative studies of the Slovenian and Scottish intermediaries. On the one hand, if R&D is dominant, BD can become neglected, resulting in a poorly developed path to market and loss of competitive advantage. On the other hand, if exclusively BD-support interventions constitute innovation policy, then the level and quality of R&D can stagnate, which can bring about loss of competitive advantage as competitors develop more advanced R&D activity—especially in the fast-paced high-tech domains (Parikh 2001).

In summary, the classification and typology proposed can expose policy and operational foci which are useful to understand when developing an academic or practical assessment of innovation intermediation provision in an ecosystem. This analysis exemplifies the kind of insight that can be garnered from heuristic deployment of the proposed model, both on the level of interventions' classification (resources/activities, physical/social, systemic/direct), the contextual factors (close involvement, systemic investment, soft leadership and strong mandate) as well as the typology of intermediaries' roles (enablers, equippers, shapers and movers).

Crucially, analysis of this sort can help identify roles that intermediary organisations play and expose gaps in the support available. In particular, a careful examination can expose assumptions and path-dependencies that lead to imbalances in the intervention development, which policymakers may need to address in order to build a more holistic policy mix of approaches. These are critical considerations, as failure to develop a well-balanced and sustainable innovation intermediation programme may lead in the long term to loss of competitive advantage through weakened BD or R&D capacity. In the next chapter, we examine the tools policymakers, innovation intermediaries' managers and entrepreneurs can use to develop, deploy and fully utilise a comprehensive combination of interventions.

Bibliography

Asheim, B. T. (2013). Smart Specialisation—Old Wine in New Bottles or New Wine in Old Bottles? In *ERSA Conference Papers*.

Azar, C., & Sandén, B. A. (2011). The Elusive Quest for Technology-Neutral Policies. *Environmental Innovation and Societal Transitions, 1*, 135–139. https://doi.org/10.1016/j.eist.2011.03.003.

Bennett, R. (2008). SME Policy Support in Britain Since the 1990s: What Have We Learnt? *Environment and Planning C: Government and Policy, 26*, 375–397. https://doi.org/10.1068/c07118.

Blair, R. (2002). Policy Tools Theory and Implementation Networks: Understanding State Enterprise Zone Partnerships. *Journal of Public Administration Research and Theory, 12*, 161–190. https://doi.org/10.1093/oxfordjournals.jpart.a003528.

Boschma, R. (2013). *Constructing Regional Advantage and Smart Specialization: Comparison of Two European Policy Concepts* (No. 13.22). Papers in Evolutionary Economic Geography, Utrecht.

Boschma, R., & Frenken, K. (2011). Technological Relatedness, Related Variety and Economic Geography. In P. Cooke, B. T. Asheim, R. Boschma, R. Martin, D. Schwartz, & F. Tdtling (Eds.), *Handbook of Regional Innovation and Growth* (pp. 187–197). London: Edward Elgar Publishing. https://doi.org/10.1093/jeg/lbq053.

Bucar, M. (2015). *Stairway to Excellence Country Report: Slovenia*. https://doi.org/10.2791/121910.

Bučar, M., & Rissola, G. (2018). *Place-Based Innovation Ecosystems: Ljubljana Start-Up Ecosystem and the Technology Park Ljubljana (Slovenia)*. Brussels. https://doi.org/10.2760/717413.

Edler, J., Cunningham, P., Gök, A., & Shapira, P. (2013). Impacts of Innovation Policy: Synthesis and Conclusions. (Report prepared as part of the project "Compendium of Evidence on the Effectiveness of Innovation Policy Intervention." (NESTA)). Manchester: Manchester Institute of Innovation Research.

Farole, T., Rodríguez-Pose, A., & Storper, M. (2010). Human Geography and the Institutions That Underlie Economic Growth. *Progress in Human Geography, 35*, 58–80. https://doi.org/10.1177/0309132510372005.

Flanagan, K., Uyarra, E., & Laranja, M. (2011). Reconceptualising the 'Policy Mix' for Innovation. *Research Policy, 40*, 702–713. https://doi.org/10.1016/j.respol.2011.02.005.

Gross, R., Blyth, W., & Heptonstall, P. (2010). Risks, Revenues and Investment in Electricity Generation: Why Policy Needs to Look Beyond Costs. *Energy Economics*. https://doi.org/10.1016/j.eneco.2009.09.017.

HM Government. (2017). *Industrial Strategy: Building a Britain Fit for the Future*. London.

Hyysalo, S., & Stewart, J. (2008). Intermediaries, Users and Social Learning in Technological Innovation. *International Journal of Innovation Management, 12*, 295–325. https://doi.org/10.1142/S1363919608002035.

Kerry, C., & Danson, M. (2016). Open Innovation, Triple Helix and Regional Innovation Systems. *Industry and Higher Education, 30*, 67–78. https://doi.org/10.5367/ihe.2016.0292.

Kivimaa, P. (2014). Government-Affiliated Intermediary Organisations as Actors in System-Level Transitions. *Research Policy, 43*, 1370–1380. https://doi.org/10.1016/j.respol.2014.02.007.

Ngwenya, H., & Hagmann, J. (2011). Making Innovation Systems Work in Practice: Experiences in Integrating Innovation, Social Learning and Knowledge in Innovation Platforms. *Knowledge Management for Development Journal, 7*, 109–124. https://doi.org/10.1080/19474199.2011.593867.

Nishimura, J., & Okamuro, H. (2011). Subsidy and Networking: The Effects of Direct and Indirect Support Programs of the Cluster Policy. *Research Policy, 40*, 714–727. https://doi.org/10.1016/J.RESPOL.2011.01.011.

Parikh, M. (2001). Knowledge Management Framework for High-Tech Research and Development. *Engineering Management Journal, 13*, 27–34. https://doi.org/10.1080/10429247.2001.11415124.

Radosevic, S., & Myrzakhmet, M. (2009). Between Vision and Reality: Promoting Innovation Through Technoparks in an Emerging Economy. *Technovation, 29*, 645–656. https://doi.org/10.1016/J.TECHNOVATION.2009.04.001.

Regulation (EC) No 1059/2003 of the European Parliament and of the Council of 26 May 2003 on the Establishment of a Common Classification of Territorial Units for Statistics (NUTS). (2018). European Parliament, Brussels.

Stare, M., Bucar, M., & Udovic, B. (2014). Soustvarjanje znanja med javnimi raziskovalnimi organizacijami in gospodarstvom za povecanje konkurencnosti. *IB Revija, 3–4*, 53–59.

Valdaliso, J. M., Magro, E., Navarro, M., Aranguren, M. J., & Wilson, J. R. (2014). Path Dependence in Policies Supporting Smart Specialisation Strategies Insights from the Basque Case. *European Journal of Innovation Management, 17*, 390–408. https://doi.org/10.1108/EJIM-12-2013-0136.

Vidmar, M. (2019a). The Ten Million Euro Question: How Do Innovation Intermediaries Support Smart Specialization? *Croatian Economic Survey, 21*, 37–84.

Vidmar, M. (2019b). Agile Space Living Lab—The Emergence of a New High-Tech Innovation Paradigm. *Space Policy, 49*. 101324

Vidmar, M. (2020). New Space and Innovation Policy: Scotland's Emerging "Space Glen". *New Space, 8*, 31–51. https://doi.org/10.1089/space.2019.0032.

Vidmar, M. (2021). Enablers, Equippers, Shapers and Movers: A typology of innovation intermediaries interventions and the development of an emergent innovation system. *Acta Astronautica, 179*, 280–289.

Willetts, D. (2013). *8 Great Technologies, 2013.* London: Policy Exchange.

CHAPTER 6

Toolkit for Developing and Analysing Innovation Intermediaries' Interventions

Abstract This chapter outlines the implications of the proposed new model of innovation intermediation for further research, as well as proposes tools and approaches to implementing its insights in practice. The latter covers both macro-level policymaking as well as developing specific innovation intermediaries and interventions. Based on work with Innovation Caucus and other projects, a clear set of guidelines is proposed to show how the necessity for a holistic approach to innovation intermediation presented here can be translated into innovation policy. Furthermore, use of structural tools, such as logic models, to operationalise the proposed classification and typology when designing new interventions is developed. Finally, to further research and practice, opportunities are explored to map the synergies between policy and its implementation and the wider innovation management and entrepreneurial learning contexts.

Keywords Innovation policy • Organisational learning • Innovation management • Entrepreneurship • Logic models • Quantified correlated impacts

The classification proposed in this book and its typological analysis is meant to address critical issues in developing innovation intermediaries and their interventions. Hence, there are specific insights that can be

M. Vidmar, *Innovation Intermediaries and (Final) Frontiers of High-tech*, https://doi.org/10.1007/978-3-030-60642-8_6

applied in policymaking, operational management and in the establishment of a new entrepreneurial mind-set. In particular, the framing of impact and performance measurement in innovation policy can be aided by understanding the intervention classes and their connections to contextual factors and typological organisational roles. Similarly, innovation intermediaries' managers can use tools like logic models, key performance indicators and contextual benchmarks to design, evaluate and evolve the deployed programmes. Finally, understanding the implications of innovation intermediation on the wider ecosystem can help entrepreneurs, policymakers and intermediaries' managers alike to appreciate the most meaningful ways to engage with each other.

As the economic policy is becoming increasingly tied in with the advances in science and technology, innovation support emerged as a key instrument of economic development. In particular, inter-organisational translation and brokerage are recognised as vital contributions to innovation intermediation, with a view to strengthening the systemic capacity for turning new knowledge into commercial products and services. This is in particular related to the concept of open innovation—the notion that new products and services are developed within an interdisciplinary context where ideas and outcomes flow across organisational boundaries (Chesbrough 2006). The links between the desired outcomes back to interventions and even further to the investment required can be used for ensuring coherence in the policymaking process.

There is an additional implication that often publicly-funded science and technology R&D is required to generate an (economic) impact on the wider society. As delivering such impact through open innovation translat ion/commercialisation of basic research into business ventures requires a bringing together of a variety of stakeholders—academia, businesses, commercial services, regulators and so on—this is sometimes referred to as the triple helix. Having to engage a multiplicity of partners and their competing interests as well as the need to meet expectations derived from governmental/public support, intermediaries are often required to justify and measure the effects of their interventions. Hence, there are significant requirements for intervention design and evaluation, including the development of business models for their operations, key performance indicators to assess their success and a logic model explaining the theory of change linking the two. Here, too, the proposed model can be useful to develop intervention programmes based on evidence, as well as use the classification and typological understanding to measure and present impact assessments.

The implementations of such interventions are also generating societal impacts beyond immediate business formation. In particular, entrepreneurial ecosystems often emerge around sustained open innovation initiatives. These are linked to a wider innovation culture related to places of intra- and inter-organisational learning and collaborative project work. This spans from skills in technology and innovation management to business development insights and organisational processes. Understanding the more open and semi-stable configurations of the various players in the ecosystem can be particularly helpful to expand on the types of interventions suitable to supporting them. For instance, the Scottish New Space sector's Agile Space Living Lab (Vidmar 2019a) requires a systemic appreciation of the enabling factors behind its success (e.g. highly skilled workforce, research infrastructure, etc.) and the required support to maintain them competitive.

Policy Implications: Navigating Holistic Approaches to Emerging Innovation Systems

The impact is becoming a central theme in science policy in the developed world, especially in traditional research-intensive countries, such as the UK. Since the beginning of the 2000s, there has been a significant refocusing of the nature of political support—and crucially funding—for basic science. This marked a shift from "research for the sake of knowledge" rationale towards the "economic case" view (Power 2000), though such arguments were inherently present since the "industrialisation of science" during and after Second World War (Nelson 1959).

This is underwritten by three trends: firstly the privileged status of science in society was undermined by its connection to industrial warfare in the mid-twentieth century and consequent politicisation of science through state or corporate interests; secondly, the neoliberal state emerging since the 1980s significantly changed the public finance landscape, towards target-driven funding; and thirdly, the scientific method in many of the core natural sciences has moved from the "investigator-driven" and individual-centred research towards "mission-driven" (Esparza and Yamada 2007), capital-intensive, global projects, involving a large community of (distributed) researchers. This is also known as Big Science (De Solla Price 1963; Weinberg 1961), a term which is now commonly used to denote large scientific projects and key institutions in natural sciences, most significantly in Physics. These projects are associated with a significant investment of capital and human resources (Heilbron and Seidel 1989) and are most often transcending rigid definitions of scientific disciplines and institutional or even national borders (Gallison and Hevly 1992). In the 2010s, in the European Union alone, €10 bn was spent annually on running large shared research facilities (Barker et al. 2013).

The economic case justification of the scale of investment in such Big Science projects is mainly centred on the premise that these complex systems, of which research organisations and collaborations are part of, are near synonymous with innovation and technological advancement (Jacob and Hallonsten 2012; Scarrà and Piccaluga 2020). In this sense, technological innovation is listed as de facto one of the key research outputs (Pavitt 1991) and often the main factor in estimating the impact of these large publicly funded research programmes (Salter and Martin 2001), which is essential for successful lobbying for (further) public funds (Bozeman 2000; Kinsella 1996).

On a global scale, perhaps no other Big Science investment regularly receives as much attention as Space Science and Exploration. In many ways, the technological developments from the advances in this field (mainly in the US) had more profound effects on society than the exploration achievements themselves (Comstock and Lockney 2007). Hence, significant and increasing importance is placed on innovation and commercialisation (micro-)management within such endeavours, but the theoretical understanding of this is often limited and lacking.

Here, understanding of innovation intermediation is vital, since it is often the mechanism of interdisciplinary and inter-organisational translation of new knowledge and technology. In this vein, the systematisation of the options for innovation intermediation support that can be deployed to facilitate such work is a welcome addition to the policymakers' toolkit. In particular, the understanding of the links between deploying political and financial capital to shore up the necessary resources enabling intermediaries' programmes and the intended outcomes of the interventions to support innovation can be used to great advantage in the design of policies.

Innovation Caucus Briefing Notes

The innovation intermediation interventions framework presented in this book was developed from the beginning with policymakers in mind. First drafts of the classification, engagement typology and conceptual logic model were prepared as part of a project through Innovation Caucus, an initiative co-funded by Innovate UK and Economic and Social Research Council (both are now part of UK Research and Innovation).

In particular, to assist in Innovate UK's review of their flagship programmes, the classification was mapped against the activities of the Catapult network of business accelerators and the interconnecting Knowledge Transfer Networks (KTNs).

As a result, two briefing notes were produced to assist Innovate UK in setting out their policy approach to innovation intermediation provisions as well as support intermediaries' managers (of individual Catapult accelerators) with the deployment of their interventions. This way of thinking and planning interventions was found particularly helpful when designing intermediaries' key performance indicators, as is explored in the next section, as well as with provision (gap) analysis, as shown in Chap. 5.

Specifically, looking at the correspondence of intervention classes to contextual factors, policy can be built around strategic decisions as to the priority needs in geo-sectoral context. As per the analysis presented earlier in Chap. 4, deployment of financial, political, social and human capital brings about interventions based on systemic investment, enactment of strong vision/mandate, soft leadership or close involvement respectively. Hence, policymakers can work backwards from the desired interventions to allocate required resources and vice versa when resources are pre-determined.

Given the implied evolutionary trajectory embedded into the typology, intervention strategies can account for the level of comparative development and be shaped to build and change over time. For example, findings indicate that in an emerging sector there is a greater need for close involvement whilst when progressing towards maturity there is more of soft leadership. This means that initially resources should be allocated to focus on intermediaries employing staff to support space and knowledge management and engage with companies directly through supporting their innovation projects.

However, as the geo-sectoral context develops, supported intermediaries should prioritise providing more specialised support, by either being given a more prominent public role and associated political capital) and/or (re)direct budget to invest in critical infrastructure and/or skills development. Although if the stage of the geo-sectoral development merits it, intermediaries can also start directly with interventions enacting a strong vision/mandate and/or providing systemic investment.

When it comes to engaging in soft leadership, intermediaries require a track record of presence in the geo-sectoral context to have the social capital needed to pull it off. If a sector is deemed mature enough that only interventions engaging with soft leadership are required, but new intermediaries are being set up, then policymakers should make provision for them to be staffed with recognised leaders in the field with extensive networks. These staff can be either from existing but less prominent organisations or from different geo-sectoral context.

It is important to note that throughout policy development, a detailed analysis of geo-sectoral context is needed to determine what are the ecosystems' requirements. As seen in the case study presented in Chap. 5, direct questions about the needs of various stakeholders can be asked to robustly determine which classes of interventions are most needed and which are less relevant (or even overprovided). It is also important that policy intentions have to be translated well into operational plans. In particular, innovation intermediaries' managers require tools to develop, monitor and assess interventions in a robust and reliable way.

Implementation Implications: Interventions, Theories of Change and Logic Models

Whilst the new classification and the corresponding typology are in of themselves useful analytical tools, in order to operationalise them in innovation intermediation practice, they need to be integrated into strategic instruments used by managers and policymakers. In particular, the logic of any intervention resulting in the desired outcome needs to be laid out explicitly in relation to the underlying theory of change (Clark and Taplin 2012). A tool often used for such planning is logic models, which are a quick schematic way to show the intended pathway from inputs (such as financial and human resources, knowledge, social/political capital) through activities (i.e. interventions) and their outputs towards the desired outcomes or impact. The exact relationship between these elements is then often captured with so-called Key Performance Indicators (KPIs), i.e.

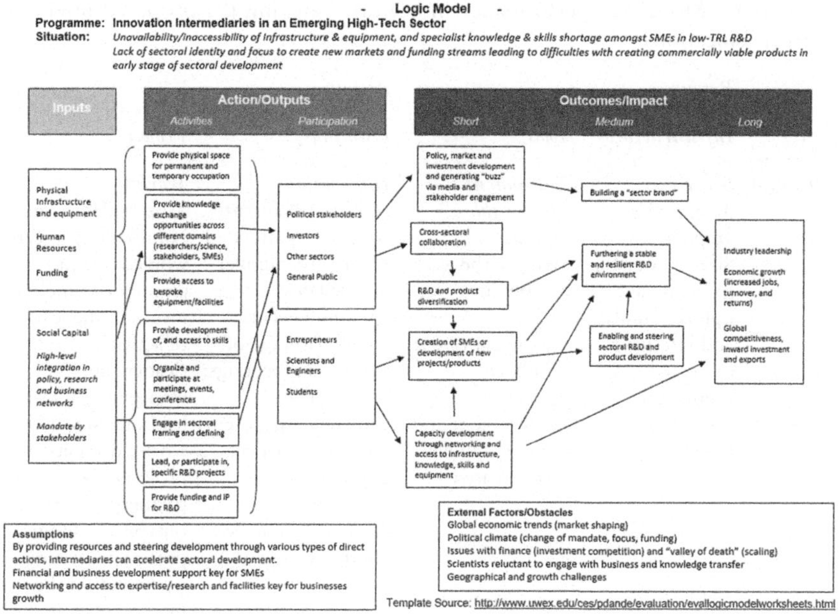

Fig. 6.1 A speculative logic model outlining the theory of change between the intervention classes, required resources and the predicted and desired outcomes/impacts

the intended outputs of an intervention programme. These are set as targets or goals of the interventions and are often measured quantitatively. A hypothetical logic model for the interventions' classification presented in this book can be seen in Fig. 6.1.

This mock model outlines the proposed theory of change based on the deployment of the eight classes of innovation intermediaries' interventions, showing the required input of their relevant contextual factors, and defines a non-exhaustive series of desired outcomes/impacts. The latter are always subject to policy intentions or the framework of the evaluation exercise, and can vary significantly even within the deployment of the same classes of interventions. Critically, the identification of desired outcomes has to be supported by evidence—as per the extensive review of literature on each class in Chap. 4. Once the target outcomes are defined, then the corresponding measurement of outputs from the interventions can be selected amongst all available KPIs. As an example, an indicative, but by no means exhaustive, list of relevant KPIs was drawn alongside the proposed framework, as seen in Table 6.1.

Table 6.1 Model key performance indicators matching the proposed interventions classifications

	Resources		*Activities*	
	Infrastructure	*Tools*	*Framing*	*Project*
Physical	***Space*** *Measurable outputs:* Size of available space; tenant uptake; number and frequency of hosted events; the impact of hosted events	***Equipment*** *Measurable outputs:* Value of the equipment; frequency of use; the impact of use on R&D projects; development and value of any new tools created	***Interaction*** *Measurable outputs:* Number of attended events; the number of delegates attending events; media coverage of events and meetings; high-profile endorsements; event outcomes (papers, reports, further meetings, partnerships made, contracts signed)	***Work*** *Measurable outputs:* Number of projects worked on; the amount of time invested; the level of activity (leadership, management, task leads, technical work); diversity of projects and partners; project outcomes (design, prototype, testing, a product on the market, revenue generated, business turnover)
Social	***Knowledge*** *Measurable outputs:* Number of papers published; citation impact; licensing/use of patents; use of mapping and database tools	***Skills*** *Measurable outputs:* Number of hours and (monetary value) of hired expertise; the number of attendees at training programmes; the number of informal partners; the number of outreach and recruitment events and their impact	***Translation*** *Measurable outputs:* Number of policy papers and briefings; the impact of policy activities (changes to regulation, investment, etc.); involvement in standardisation processes (role, quality of engagement and impact); number and impact of media publications and appearances	***Capital*** *Measurable outputs:* Value of the financial investment in projects; the value of IP or in-kind investment in project; the impact of project promotion (within the network, in policy or financial arena and in the media); the success of the backed projects (project outcomes as in the box above)

Here, the focus on intervention classification, rather than intermediaries' roles, is helpful by making the structural features of intermediation easily translatable in operational practice. By understanding the mix of resources available to an intermediary, intervention classes can be developed and deployed to suit the context and proposed outcomes. For instance, the resources can be grouped along the contextual factors of having staff and capital capacity for close involvement, financial backing for systemic investment, political/social standing for enacting a strong vision/mandate and kudos, skills and networks to exude thought leadership.

Once the resources are well understood, matching intervention classes can be looked at to arrange a suitable mix to address the expected outcomes within the ecosystem. This is obviously going to be very much case-specific, however many emerging high-tech geo-sectoral contexts may find intermediaries converging on the typology outlined in this book, with enablers, equippers, shapers and movers, as resources availability and political/public expectations seem to converge in most Western countries.

In order to relate achieving KPIs to desired intervention outcomes or impacts, an interpretive framework needs to be deployed. Such frameworks often operate on the basis of cost to benefit analysis—minimising the interventions' programme cost whilst maximising the impact. However, these analyses are often challenging as it is difficult to unpick the effect of a specific intervention from all other activities within the ecosystem—referred to as the attribution—as well as assess what would be the likely outcome without intervention, i.e. a counterfactual analysis (Ferraro 2009). Hence, multiple frameworks have emerged to address these challenges, such as the Quantified Correlated Impacts (QCI).

Quantified Correlated Impacts (QCI)

The QCI framework is being developed to address the methodological uncertainty often accompanying impact evaluation exercises in science, technology and innovation interventions (Autio 2014; Markman et al. 2008; Zuijdam et al. 2011). It is being derived empirically from understanding the needs of evaluators and other stakeholders as well as their current practices, for instance, that of UK Research and Innovation funding bodies.

(*continued*)

(continued)

At the core of this approach lies an interlinked bundle of quantitative and qualitative methods (Datta 1997). The quantitative data about the outputs of a programme on the sample are linked with the qualitative assessment to the proportionate impact the intervention has had. This is measured as a contribution to the total difference between key pre-defined parameters in the sample and the correlated trends in the wider population.

Said parameters are the key outcomes as set in the logic model (University of Wisconsin-Madison 2020), which is linking the intervention from the inputs required through the action taken to the impacts generated, whilst this path, or logic, is supported by evidence (Rossi et al. 2003). This is broadly still an instance of cost-benefit analysis, where the input of resources is compared to the positive effects of the intervention, however, it is moving away from the often contested simplicity of quantitative data (Cellini and Kee 2010) into a mixed-method approach, wary of the multitude of factors affecting the outcomes and the often subjective benchmarking of success (Datta 1997).

The framework is based on two premises: on the one hand, the need for quantified data useful in public policy arena (Barker 1994), and on the other hand, the need for moderation and analysis of that data by the very actors it concerns (Nutley et al. 2007, p. 486). This latter part is crucial to estimate the contribution any particular intervention has had to a multitude of complex factors present in the socio-economic sphere and for identification of which background trends are relevant to benchmark against.

Using such framework is useful for both developing a contextual understanding of the performance of an intervention programme and expanding on the narrowly defined monetary impacts, to include other societal and environmental benefits, whilst maintaining evidential rigour. The latter is particularly useful in lobbying for continuous financial and/or political support.

In addition, use of well-structured tools like QCI combined with their scope for qualitative/ethnographic contextualisation can lead to the identification of unexpected/unintended outcomes and factors contributing to the success or failure of interventions. It can also expose underlying trends and the role intermediaries and their interventions play in them. For example, one such critical dimension of intermediation, which is hard to quantify or even qualify otherwise, is the development of an entrepreneurial mind-set and culture as will be explored in the next section.

Higher Education Institutions and Innovation Intermediation[1]
Higher Education Institutions (HEIs) often play a vital intermediation role in the entrepreneurial ecosystem spanning several critical classes of interventions. As an example, a model for HEIs' support for entrepreneurship was designed by the Organisation for Economic Cooperation and Development (OECD) within the HEInnovate initiative, based on eight dimensions:

- Leadership and governance
- Organisational capacity: funding, people and incentives
- Entrepreneurial teaching and learning
- Preparing and supporting entrepreneurs
- Digital transformation and capability
- Knowledge exchange and collaboration
- The internationalised institution
- Measuring impact

Examining the context of entrepreneurial culture in particular—that is, the fourth dimension of preparing and supporting the entrepreneurs—led to the articulation of six key framework action areas to prepare and support entrepreneurs:

1. The HEI increases awareness of the value of entrepreneurship and stimulates the entrepreneurial intentions of students, graduates and staff to start up a business or venture.

(*continued*)

[1] The importance of HEI within the context of innovation intermediation was explored by the author within the context of helping prepare HEInnovate report in the state of entrepreneurial university framework conditions in Romania (OECD/European Commission 2019).

(continued)

2. The HEI supports its students, graduates and staff to move from idea generation to business creation.
3. Training is offered to assist students, graduates and staff in starting, running and growing a business.
4. Mentoring and other forms of personal development are offered by experienced individuals from academia or industry.
5. The HEI facilitates access to financing for its entrepreneurs.
6. The HEI offers or facilitates access to business incubation.

These activities quite closely mirror the intervention classes outlined in this book, in particular in developing skills, supporting translation and facilitating access to capital and space respectively.

More details about this framework and associated tools for examining and improving upon framework conditions with an HEI or its environment can be found at www.heinovate.org

Ecosystem Implications: Co-evolving Innovation and Entrepreneurial Culture

Organisational and entrepreneurial learning is often opportunistic and stochastic. However, patterns and trends do emerge around instances of sectoral clustering, the external pressures of funding and market access, as well as through business development support, including innovation intermediation.

An example from researching innovation in the emerging New Space sector in Scotland is the development of structural absorptive capacity amongst SMEs by adopting approaches from cognitively proximate domains, for example the IT industry, and then spreading them along the New Space value chain (Vidmar 2020). As evidence shows, innovation intermediaries are crucial for the value chain integration since they play a key part in defining the shape and scope of entrepreneurial and inter-organisational networks, which facilitate learning and capacity development.

As an underscore to the systemic and cultural nature of organisational learning, New Space companies have also often adopted features of IT firms' culture such as dress code, social events and interior design.

Most (Scottish) New Space companies, whether IT-related or not, have very relaxed working spaces with employees wearing informal clothes (jeans, t-shirts, sweaters, etc.), organise regular social events for all staff and have installed kitchens/bars and recreation/relaxation areas. Hence, there are significant implications of a better understanding of innovation intermediaries' interventions and the development of an entrepreneurial culture, especially how entrepreneurs and their organisations get developed. Of particular significance here are intermediation activities carried out in and around higher education institutions, as championed in the OECD's HEInnovate framework.

Furthermore, innovation intermediaries are critical in developing interdisciplinary and collaborative interactions, which often permeates all types of interventions. As an example, physical colocation of innovation partners/stakeholders and development of platform solutions for managing R&D processes has been seen as a crucial part of entrepreneurial mindset development supporting open innovation processes. One particularly dominant paradigm is the Living Laboratory conceptualisation of developing a networked, project-centred environment to align various stakeholders towards common innovation goals.

The Making of a Living Lab

The framing of Living Laboratories has built on the ideas of innovation (eco)systems, R&D clusters and the triple-helix model of research exploitation, as briefly touched upon in Chap. 2. Specifically, the Living Labs approach (Almirall et al. 2012; Feurstein et al. 2008; Følstad 2008) has proposed that "innovation laboratory" is increasingly located neither in the company, nor in the university, nor in the government, nor in the public sphere, but in the in-between space of networked interactions.

Interestingly, most of such "laboratories" are developed and managed by innovation intermediary organisations who facilitate the bringing together of different stakeholders with varied areas of expertise and interests before embarking on managed processes of discovering an opportunity for collaborative work. These configurations of actors and innovation environments are deliberately built, but they critically rely on enabling contexts. For instance, based on recent research, Scotland has a great potential for Living

(*continued*)

(continued)
Lab innovation, as it contains the natural and social environment supportive of a socio-economic bounding (stakeholder identification), presents a diverse natural and social environment (needed for in-situ innovation contextualisation), has R&D capacity through research institutions and intermediaries (needed for project management) and has a significant user base (highly-skilled workforce and population) (Vidmar 2019a).

Within a Living Lab, specific projects can be developed via innovation intermediaries deploying R&D management capacity, which supports the configuration of stakeholders and stabilisation of socio-economically viable relationships. In particular, intermediaries can provide interaction, translation and work-type interventions to help stakeholders working together to develop cross-cutting interests and projects that can fill the demand derived from these processes. More detail on developing Living Lab methodology modelled on this principles was published in a report on the evolution of the Edinburgh Living Lab (Vidmar 2019b).

In summary, innovation intermediaries' interventions give rise to a complex landscape of effects in developing and supporting innovation and entrepreneurial activity. Through helping establish an open innovation and dynamic entrepreneurial culture, organisations such as higher education institutions and dedicated public agencies can encourage organisational learning leading to an increase in competitiveness within a Geographically-Bound Sectoral System of Innovation, in particular, in the high-tech domains.

Bibliography

Almirall, E., Lee, M., & Wareham, J. (2012). Mapping Living Labs in the Landscape of Innovation Methodologies. *Technology Innovation and Management Review, 2*, 12–18. https://doi.org/10.22215/timreview/603.

Autio, E. (2014). *Innovation from Big Science: Enhancing Big Science Impact Agenda*. London: Department of Business, Innovation and Skill.

Barker, K. (1994). Strengthening the Impact of R&D Evaluation on Policy Making: Methodological and Organisational Considerations. *Science and Public Policy, 21*, 405–413. https://doi.org/10.1093/spp/21.6.405.

Barker, K., Sveinsdottir, T., & Cox, D. (2013). The "Innovation Turn" in Policy for Large Scientific Facilities: Reflections on Introducing Innovation Support Dimensions to the Operation of Scientific Research Infrastructure. In *EU-SPRI* (p. 37). Madrid.

Bozeman, B. (2000). Technology Transfer and Public Policy: A Review of Research and Theory. *Research Policy, 29*, 627–655. https://doi.org/10.1016/S0048-7333(99)00093-1.

Cellini, S. R., & Kee, J. E. (2010). Cost-Effectiveness and Cost-Benefit Analysis. In J. S. Wholey, H. P. Hatry, & K. E. Newcomer (Eds.), *Handbook of Practical Program Evaluation* (pp. 493–530). San Francisco: Jossey-Bass.

Chesbrough, H. (2006). Innovation Intermediaries Enabling Open innovation. In *Open Business Models: How to Thrive in the New Innovation Landscape* (p. 33). https://doi.org/10.1107/S1600536808017583.

Clark, H., & Taplin, D. (2012). *Theory of Change Basics: A Primer on Theory of Change, ActKnowledge*. New York: Actknowledge. https://doi.org/10.5327/Z201600010002RBM.

Comstock, D. A., & Lockney, D. (2007). NASA's Legacy of Technology Transfer and Prospects for Future Benefits. In *A Collection of Technical Papers—AIAA Space 2007 Conference* (pp. 2969–2978). https://doi.org/10.2514/6.2007-6283.

Datta, L. (1997). Multimethod Evaluations: Using Case Studies Together with Other Methods. In W. R. Shadish & E. Chelimsky (Eds.), *Evaluation for the 21st Century: A Handbook* (pp. 344–360). Thousand Oaks: Sage.

De Solla Price, D. (1963). *Big Science, Little Science*. New York: Columbia University.

Esparza, J., & Yamada, T. (2007). The Discovery Value of "Big Science". *The Journal of Experimental Medicine, 204*, 701–704. https://doi.org/10.1084/jem.20070073.

Ferraro, P. J. (2009). Counterfactual Thinking and Impact Evaluation in Environmental Policy. *New Directions for Evaluation, 2009*, 75–84. https://doi.org/10.1002/ev.297.

Feurstein, K., Hesmer, A., Hribernik, K. A., Thoben, K. D., & Schumacher, J. (2008). Living Labs: A New Development Strategy. In *European Living Labs-a New Approach for Human Centric Regional Innovation*. Berlin: Wissenschaftlicher Verlag.

Følstad, A. (2008). Living Labs for Innovation and Development of Information and Communication Technology: A Literature Review. *The Electronic Journal for Virtual Organizations and Networks, 10*, 99–131.

Gallison, P., & Hevly, B. (1992). *Big Science: The Growth of Large-Scale Research*. New York: Stanford University Press.

Heilbron, J. L., & Seidel, R. W. (1989). *Lawrence and His Laboratory: A History of the Lawrence Berkeley Laboratory*. https://doi.org/10.1088/0004-637X/710/1/634.

Jacob, M., & Hallonsten, O. (2012). The Persistence of Big Science and Megascience in Research and Innovation Policy. *Science and Public Policy, 39*, 411–415. https://doi.org/10.1093/scipol/scs056.

Kinsella, W. (1996). A "Fusion" of Interests: Big Science, Government, and Rhetorical Practice in Nuclear Fusion Research. *Rhetoric Society Quarterly, 26*, 65–81. https://doi.org/10.1080/02773949609391079.

Markman, G. D., Siegel, D. S., & Wright, M. (2008). Research and Technology Commercialization. *Journal of Management Studies, 45*, 1401–1423. https://doi.org/10.1111/j.1467-6486.2008.00803.x.

Nelson, R. R. (1959). The Simple Economics of Basic Scientific Research. *Journal of Political Economy, 67*, 297–306. https://doi.org/10.1086/258177.

Nutley, S. M., Walter, I., & Davies, H. T. O. (2007). *Using Evidence: How Research Can Inform Public Services.* London: Policy Press.

Pavitt, K. (1991). What Makes Basic Research Economically Useful? *Research Policy, 20*, 109–119. https://doi.org/10.1016/0048-7333(91)90074-Z.

Power, M. (2000). The Audit Society—Second Thoughts. *International Journal of Auditing, 4*, 111–119.

Rossi, P., Lipsey, M., & Freeman, H. (2003). *Evaluation: A Systematic Approach* (7th ed.). London: Sage.

Salter, A. J., & Martin, B. R. (2001). The Economic Benefits of Publicly Funded Basic Research: A Critical Review. *Research Policy, 30*, 509–532. https://doi.org/10.1016/S0048-7333(00)00091-3.

Scarrà, D., & Piccaluga, A. (2020). The Impact of Technology Transfer and Knowledge Spillover from Big Science: A Literature Review. *Technovation*, 102165. https://doi.org/10.1016/j.technovation.2020.102165.

OECD/European Commission (2019). Supporting Entrepreneurship and Innovation in Higher Education in Romania. [Report] Paris: OECD

University of Wisconsin-Madison. (2020). Logic Models—Program Development and Evaluation [WWW Document]. https://fyi.extension.wisc.edu/program-development/logic-models/. Accessed 6 July 2020.

Vidmar, M. (2019a). Agile Space Living Lab—The Emergence of a New High-Tech Innovation Paradigm. *Space Policy, 49*. 101324

Vidmar, M. (2019b). *The "Living Lab" Method: Discovery > Challenge > Innovation.* Edinburgh. https://doi.org/10.13140/RG.2.2.21744.20484.

Vidmar, M., Rosiello, A., Vermeulen, N., Williams, R., & Dines, J. (2020). New space and agile innovation: Understanding transition to open innovation by examining innovation networks and moments. *Acta astronautica, 167*, 122–134.

Weinberg, A. M. (1961). Impact of Large-Scale Science on the United States. *Science, 134*, 161–164. https://doi.org/10.1126/science.134.3473.161.

Zuijdam, F., Boekholt, P., Deuten, J., Meijer, I., & Vermeulen, N. (2011). *The Role and Added Value of Large-Scale Research Facilities.* Amsterdam: Technopolis Group.

CHAPTER 7

Conclusion

Abstract This conclusion summarises the main findings and arguments presented in this book and reiterates the need for a comprehensive understanding of innovation intermediaries' interventions and their roles in innovation processes and in policymaking. It further proposes some policy directions for the studied context, the New Space sector in peripheral countries, crucially in Scotland, as well as making final observations about the evolving nature of innovation intermediation, with particular reference to recent digitisation of the activities involved and likely policy agenda in the post-Covid-19 pandemic era.

Keywords Policy recommendations • Future research • Covid-19

The analysis presented in this book examined the current state of the art in the innovation intermediaries' literature, especially related to high-tech open-innovation-driven economic development policy, as outlined in detail in the Introduction (Chap. 1). Through a systematic literature review of the recent empirical work in innovation intermediation, the tendency amongst researchers to frame their work in a geographically and sectoral bounded cases was noted. Hence, Geographically-Bound Sectoral Systems of Innovation (GSSI) framing was proposed as the de facto analytical unit for comprehensive analysis of innovation intermediation. This literature survey also reiterated some of the most persistent challenges for

M. Vidmar, *Innovation Intermediaries and (Final) Frontiers of High-tech*, https://doi.org/10.1007/978-3-030-60642-8_7

analysts and practitioners alike, namely an acute lack of integration of various theories and meaningful systematisation of available actions, which often leads to poor application of state-of-the-art insights. Based on these insights, this book set to remodel innovation intermediation understanding to address functional and analytical gaps and divisions. This led to a five-step theoretical and empirical examination and development of conceptual and operational framing of innovation intermediation, grounded within the study of the New Space sector in Scotland.

Firstly, Chap. 2 showed that the specific focusing on functional distinctions in the analysis of innovation intermediaries causes most problems. Examining the prevalence of knowledge borkerage as intermediary activity, the scope of the framing was extended to cover other aspects of support for innovation. In the end, an augmented pragmatic definition was adopted—the focus shifted from intermediaries as organisations towards their interventions as the main objective of the study. This is a key change of perspective, enabling a closer link between analytical systematisation of innovation intermediaries' roles and functions to their operational planning and deployment.

Secondly, as noted by many other authors and practitioners (policymakers and managers), the functional fragmentation and disconnectedness of the conceptual framework of innovation intermediation are of theoretical and practical concern. In particular, these challenges are seen to stand in the way of establishing comparative analysis of best practice in innovation intermediation, as well as leaves intermediaries without a coherent perspective on types of available tools. In Chap. 3, this was put to the test, as the understanding of innovation intermediation was explored within the example of the emerging New Space sector in Scotland. Using documentary and interview evidence of four typical cases within the Scottish New Space GSSI led to the finding that the complexity of the ground operations makes it difficult to assess and develop the intermediation provision.

Thirdly, Chap. 4 is examining the key dividing lines between systemic literature reviews (Dalziel 2010; Howells 2006; Kilelu et al. 2011; Kim 2015; Kivimaa 2014; Lukkarinen et al. 2018; Nilsson and Sia-Ljungström 2013) and additional studies. Building on these insights, this study proposed a comprehensive and inclusive classification framework based on distinctions between interventions based on the provision of resources (such as infrastructure and tools) versus deployment of activities (through framing and projects). These were further qualified with sub-categories of infrastructure, knowledge, tools and skills resources provision and activities to enable interaction, translation project work and capital. Using such a holistic classification enables theoreticians and practitioners alike to identify the systemic role of a particular intervention as well as identify a specific type of intervention in order to fulfil systemic requirements. This was expanded further by developing a proto-typology of contextual factors, noting the importance of close involvement, systemic investment, strong vision/mandate and soft leadership for the delivery of the respective intervention classes. These contextual factors were then directly linked to a series of intermediaries' roles of enabling the ecosystem, equipping the players, shaping the vision and moving the development of a sector.

Fourthly, using the case of New Space sector, the new model was deployed to (re-)examine a practical example of the innovation intermediation landscape in Chap. 5. This comprises a more detailed comparative analysis of two (largest) innovation intermediation interventions in two different geographical domains—Scotland and Slovenia as well as structural analysis of the Scottish innovation intermediation provision. The comparison of the Scottish Higgs Centre for Innovation to the Slovenian Space-SI showed that a path-dependency in the policy outlook and organisational set-up leads to diverging interventions on the ground. Specifically, Scottish intermediary focused on competitively providing business development support, whilst the Slovenian one focused on developing bespoke R&D. Such a near dichotomous split in provisions could be leading to a gradual loss of competitive advantage in both cases, so a more holistic approach to intervention design is advised. In order to understate the sum of the innovation intermediation interventions, a further aggregate analysis of needs and provision assessment is made on the four case studies within the Scottish New Space sector from Chap. 3, showing a relatively well-matched demand and supply and a critical need for direct project work (R&D) interventions.

Finally, examining the design of innovation intermediation interventions in Chap. 6, logic modelling, key performance indicators, impact assessment frameworks and the development of entrepreneurial culture were briefly outlined. Whilst not providing a complete overview of all the available tools, this chapter encourages policymakers, intermediaries' managers and entrepreneurs to look beyond the individual interventions and their effects and examine complementarities of developing a dynamic ecosystem of players supporting each other in the processes of innovation and business development. Particular role of higher education institutions is highlighted, as well as emerging new ways of collaborative working, such as the Living Laboratory framework.

Overall, this book argues for a comprehensive and holistic approach in developing, deploying, analysing and assessing innovation intermediation. The structural evolution of thinking from interventions to contextual factors and finally organisational roles can be an important unifying framework to ensure that the investment of public funds in innovation support is well thought through.

Here, several recommendations for the Scottish New Space sector are relevant, in particular the acute need for more advanced R&D investment,[1] a better understanding of the entrepreneurial culture and processes of (inter-)organisational learning, as well as a (more) strategic deployment of soft leadership (less of broad interaction, more focus on marketisation/sales). However, it is important to note the significant involvement of public actors in this sector and the potential pitfall of continuous (over) reliance on public support—that is firms receiving serial R&D grants to fund core operations rather than building revenue streams and market capitalisation. If not resolved, these issues may quickly evolve in serious challenges for maintaining competitive advantage in a global marketplace, particularly if compounded by wider economic disruption due to the Covid-19 pandemic and uncertainty of post-Brexit trade relationships.

Current limitations of this work relate to the inherent difficulty of harmonising the myriad of different frameworks, which inevitably leads to certain generalisations and omissions. Further analyses of this model, the classes, categories, contextual factors, organisations' types, linkages and the policy rationales are all very welcome, as would be its application in other high-tech sectors as well as those diverging from the high-tech paradigm. It is hoped that more such studies become available in the near future. An additional opportunity for further research lies in examining different geographical framings of sectoral development policy—either on larger national level (e.g. Vallejo et al. (2019) or more detailed (sub-) regional one (see for instance Bačić and Aralica 2017).

In particular, the current dominance of data-driven/digital innovation in the UK lends itself to further study of the new organisational dynamics within SMEs and innovation intermediation. As mentioned in the previous chapter, the culture of IT firms is seeping into other industrial sectors and spreading along the value chains to make for more lean and agile innovation processes and business operations (Birkinshaw 2020). This is a

[1] In contrast, we have seen in the limited comparison with Space-SI centre, that Slovenian policymakers should perhaps start deploying more business development interventions.

particularly interesting dynamics, within the context of the Covid-19 pandemic. On the one hand, a more widespread digitisation of more business transactions, including those previously reserved for in-person contacts such as networking and deal-making, may change the innovation culture and shift requirements for intermediation. On the other hand, the needs for offseting the required significant investment into larger scale equipment for the manufacturing processes and the need for close R&D support in emerging industrial sectors will likely remain present.

A rapid responses study actually showed that the New Space Industry (in teh UK) is quite resilient in the face of the Covid-19 challenges (Vidmar et al. 2020). Whilst this may in part be due to its existing high level of upfront investment and so far relatively low commercial market capitalisation, as a bulwark against cash flow fluctuations, the existing prevalence of digital tools and agile/lean business models also have to be noted. Thus, the sector's close interaction with innovation intermediaries and the expanse of knowledge transfer between the various actors, may have led to development of innovation processes and general business management practices that are proving vital in these turbulent times.

Bibliography

Bačić, K., & Aralica, Z. (2017). Regional Competitiveness in the Context. *Zbornik radova Ekonomskog fakulteta u Rijeci, 35*, 551–582. https://doi.org/10.18045/zbefri.2017.2.551.

Birkinshaw, J. (2020). The New Boardroom Imperative: From Agility to Resilience. *Forbes.*

Dalziel, M. (2010). Why Do Innovation Intermediaries Exist? In *Druid 2010: Opening Up Innovation: Strategy, Organization and Technology* (p. 23). London: Imperial College London Business School.

Howells, J. (2006). Intermediation and the Role of Intermediaries in Innovation. *Research Policy, 35*, 715–728. https://doi.org/10.1016/j.respol.2006.03.005.

Kilelu, C. W., Klerkx, L., Leeuwis, C., & Hall, A. (2011). Beyond Knowledge Brokering: An Exploratory Study on Innovation Intermediaries in an Evolving Smallholder Agricultural System in Kenya. *Knowledge Management for Development Journal, 7*, 84–108. https://doi.org/10.1080/19474199.2011.593859.

Kim, E. S. (2015). *Facilitating Innovation in SMEs: The Case of Public Intermediaries in South Korea* [Doctoral Thesis]. Edinburgh: The University of Edinburgh.

Kivimaa, P. (2014). Government-Affiliated Intermediary Organisations as Actors in System-Level Transitions. *Research Policy, 43*, 1370–1380. https://doi.org/10.1016/j.respol.2014.02.007.

Lukkarinen, J., Berg, A., Salo, M., Tainio, P., Alhola, K., & Antikainen, R. (2018). An Intermediary Approach to Technological Innovation Systems (TIS)—The Case of the Cleantech Sector in Finland. In *Environmental Innovation and Societal Transitions* (pp. 136–146). https://doi.org/10.1016/j.eist.2017.04.003.

Nilsson, M., & Sia-Ljungström, C. (2013, February 18–23). The Role of Innovation Intermediaries in Innovation Systems. In *2013 International European Forum* (pp. 161–180). Innsbruck/Igls: International European Forum on System Dynamics and Innovation in Food Networks.

Vallejo, B., Oyelaran-Oyeyinka, B., Ozor, N., & Bolo, M. (2019). Open Innovation and Innovation Intermediaries in Sub-Saharan Africa. *Sustainability, 11*, 392. https://doi.org/10.3390/su11020392.

Vidmar, M., Golra, O., & Rosiello, A., (2020). Resilience of New Space Firms in the UK During the Early Stages of Covid-19 Crisis: The Case for Strategic Agility. *New Space*, 8(4).

Bibliography

1st Scottish Space Symposium—University of Strathclyde [WWW Document]. (2010). https://www.strath.ac.uk/advancedspaceconceptslaboratory/newsevents/scottishspacesymposia/1stscottishspacesymposium/. Accessed 24 Dec 2018.

Abbate, T., Coppolino, R., & Schiavone, F. (2013). Linking Entities in Knowledge Transfer: The Innovation Intermediaries. *Journal of the Knowledge Economy, 4*, 233–243. https://doi.org/10.1007/s13132-013-0156-5.

Adlen, S. (2011). *Innovation in the Global Space Industry*. London: Imperial College London.

Agogué, M., Ystrom, A., & Le Masson, P. (2013). Rethinking the Role of Intermediaries as an Architect of Collective Exploration and Creation of Knowledge in Open Innovation. *International Journal of Innovation Management, 17*, 1350007. https://doi.org/10.1142/S1363919613500072.

Agogué, M., Berthet, E., Fredberg, T., Le Masson, P., Segrestin, B., Stoetzel, M., Wiener, M., & Yström, A. (2017). Explicating the Role of Innovation Intermediaries in the "Unknown": A Contingency Approach. *Journal of Strategy and Management, 10*, 19–39. https://doi.org/10.1108/JSMA-01-2015-0005.

Almirall, E., Lee, M., & Wareham, J. (2012). Mapping Living Labs in the Landscape of Innovation Methodologies. *Technology Innovation and Management Review, 2*, 12–18. https://doi.org/10.22215/timreview/603.

An Interview with the European Space Agency (ESA's) Business Incubation Centre (BIC) UK [WWW Document]. (2018). Astropreneurs. http://astropreneurs.space/2019/02/07/an-interview-with-the-european-space-agency-esas-business-incubation-centre-bic-uk/. Accessed 1 Apr 2019.

M. Vidmar, *Innovation Intermediaries and (Final) Frontiers of High-tech*, https://doi.org/10.1007/978-3-030-60642-8

Antikaninen, M., Mäkipää, M., & Ahonen, M. (2009). Motivating and Supporting Collaboration in Open Innovation. *Technology Management, 13*, 24.

Arrow, K. J. (1951). An Extension of the Basic Theorems of Classical Welfare Economics. In *Proceedings of the Second Berkeley Symposium on Mathematical Statistics and Probability* (pp. 507–532). Berkley: University of California.

Asheim, B. T. (2013). Smart Specialisation—Old Wine in New Bottles or New Wine in Old Bottles? In *ERSA Conference Papers*. European Regional Science Association.

Asheim, B. T., Smith, H. L., & Oughton, C. (2011). Regional Innovation Systems: Theory, Empirics and Policy. *Regional Studies, 45*, 875–891. https://doi.org/10.1080/00343404.2011.596701.

Autio, E. (2014). *Innovation from Big Science: Enhancing Big Science Impact Agenda*. London: Department of Business, Innovation and Skill.

Autio, E., Hameri, A. P., & Vuola, O. (2004). A Framework of Industrial Knowledge Spillovers in Big-Science Centers. *Research Policy, 33*, 107–126. https://doi.org/10.1016/S0048-7333(03)00105-7.

Autio, E., Kanninen, S., & Gustafsson, R. (2008). First- and Second-Order Additionality and Learning Outcomes in Collaborative RD Programs. *Research Policy, 37*, 59–76. https://doi.org/10.1016/J.RESPOL.2007.07.012.

Azar, C., & Sandén, B. A. (2011). The Elusive Quest for Technology-Neutral Policies. *Environmental Innovation and Societal Transitions, 1*, 135–139. https://doi.org/10.1016/j.eist.2011.03.003.

Bačić, K., & Aralica, Z. (2017). Zoran Aralica • Regional Competitiveness in the Context. *Zbornik radova Ekonomskog fakulteta u Rijeci, 35*, 551–582. https://doi.org/10.18045/zbefri.2017.2.551.

Banks, M. (2018). UK Space Sector Set for Take-Off. *Physics World, 31*, 13–13. https://doi.org/10.1088/2058-7058/31/7/20.

Barker, K. (1994). Strengthening the Impact of R&D Evaluation on Policy Making: Methodological and Organisational Considerations. *Science and Public Policy, 21*, 405–413. https://doi.org/10.1093/spp/21.6.405.

Barker, K., Sveinsdottir, T., & Cox, D. (2013). The "Innovation Turn" in Policy for Large Scientific Facilities: Reflections on Introducing Innovation Support Dimensions to the Operation of Scientific Research Infrastructure. In *EU-SPRI* (p. 37). Madrid.

Bekkers, R., & Bodas Freitas, I. M. (2008). Analysing Knowledge Transfer Channels Between Universities and Industry: To What Degree Do Sectors Also Matter? *Research Policy, 37*, 1837–1853. https://doi.org/10.1016/j.respol.2008.07.007.

Bendis, R. A., Seline, R. S., & Byler, E. J. (2008). A New Direction for Technology-Based Economic Development: The Role of Innovation Intermediaries. *Industry and Higher Education, 22*, 73–80. https://doi.org/10.5367/000000008784139460.

Bennett, R. (2008). SME Policy Support in Britain Since the 1990s: What Have We Learnt? *Environment and Planning C: Government and Policy, 26*, 375–397. https://doi.org/10.1068/c07118.

Bergek, A., Jacobsson, S., Carlsson, B., Lindmark, S., & Rickne, A. (2008). Analyzing the Functional Dynamics of Technological Innovation Systems: A Scheme of Analysis. *Research Policy, 37*, 407–429. https://doi.org/10.1016/j.respol.2007.12.003.

Bergvall-Kåreborn, B., Ihlström Eriksson, C., Ståhlbröst, A., & Lund, J. (2009). A Milieu for Innovation—Defining Living Labs. In *2nd ISPIM Innovation Symposium* (pp. 6–9). New York.

Bessant, J., & Rush, H. (1995). Building Bridges for Innovation: The Role of Consultancies in Technology Transfer. *Research Policy, 24*, 97–114. https://doi.org/10.1016/0048-7333(93)00751-E.

Birkinshaw, J. (2020). The New Boardroom Imperative: From Agility to Resilience. *Forbes*.

Blair, R. (2002). Policy Tools Theory and Implementation Networks: Understanding State Enterprise Zone Partnerships. *Journal of Public Administration Research and Theory, 12*, 161–190. https://doi.org/10.1093/oxfordjournals.jpart.a003528.

Bodas Freitas, I. M., & von Tunzelmann, N. (2008). Mapping Public Support for Innovation: A Comparison of Policy Alignment in the UK and France. *Research Policy, 37*, 1446–1464. https://doi.org/10.1016/J.RESPOL.2008.05.005.

Boon, W. P., Moors, E. H., Kuhlmann, S., & Smits, R. E. (2011). Demand Articulation in Emerging Technologies: Intermediary User Organisations as Co-Producers? *Research Policy, 40*, 242–252.

Boschma, R. (2013). *Constructing Regional Advantage and Smart Specialization: Comparison of Two European Policy Concepts* (No. 13.22). Papers in Evolutionary Economic Geography, Utrecht.

Boschma, R., & Frenken, K. (2011). Technological Relatedness, Related Variety and Economic Geography. In P. Cooke, B. T. Asheim, R. Boschma, R. Martin, D. Schwartz, & F. Tdtling (Eds.), *Handbook of Regional Innovation and Growth* (pp. 187–197). London: Edward Elgar Publishing. https://doi.org/10.1093/jeg/lbq053.

Boyns, N., Spires, R., & Cox, M. (2009). *Evaluation of Smart: Scotland*. Edinburgh: Scottish Government Social Research.

Bozeman, B. (2000). Technology Transfer and Public Policy: A Review of Research and Theory. *Research Policy, 29*, 627–655. https://doi.org/10.1016/S0048-7333(99)00093-1.

Breschi, S., & Malerba, F. (1997). Sectoral Innovation Systems: Technological Regimes, Schumpeterian Dynamics, and Spatial Boundaries. In C. Edquist (Ed.), *Systems of Innovation: Technologies, Institutions and Organizations* (pp. 130–156). Abingdon: Routledge.

Brousselle, A., & Champagne, F. (2011). Program Theory Evaluation: Logic Analysis. *Evaluation and Program Planning, 34*, 69–78. https://doi.org/10.1016/j.evalprogplan.2010.04.001.

Brown, J. S., & Duguid, P. (2001). Knowledge and Organization: A Social-Practice Perspective. *Organization Science, 12*, 198–213. https://doi.org/10.1287/orsc.12.2.198.10116.

Bucar, M. (2015). *Stairway to Excellence Country Report: Slovenia*. https://doi.org/10.2791/121910.

Bučar, M., & Rissola, G. (2018). *Place-Based Innovation Ecosystems: Ljubljana Start-Up Ecosystem and the Technology Park Ljubljana (Slovenia)*. Brussels. https://doi.org/10.2760/717413.

Bush, V. (1945). *Science: The Endless Frontier*. Washington, DC: United States Government Printing Office.

Caleb, H. (2016). OneWeb Gets $1.2 Billion in SoftBank-Led Investment. *Sp. News*.

Cellini, S. R., & Kee, J. E. (2010). Cost-Effectiveness and Cost-Benefit Analysis. In J. S. Wholey, H. P. Hatry, & K. E. Newcomer (Eds.), *Handbook of Practical Program Evaluation* (pp. 493–530). San Francisco: Jossey-Bass.

Chaminade, C., & Esquist, C. (2006). *Rationales for Public Policy Intervention in the Innovation Process: Systems of Innovation Approach, the Theory and Practice of Innovation Policy*. CIRCLE, Lund University. https://doi.org/10.4337/9781849804424.00012.

Chesbrough, H. (2003). *Open Innovation: The New Imperative for Creating and Profiting from Technology*. Boston: Harvard Business School Press.

Chesbrough, H. (2006). Innovation Intermediaries Enabling Open innovation. In *Open Business Models: How to Thrive in the New Innovation Landscape* (p. 33). https://doi.org/10.1107/S1600536808017583.

Chesbrough, H. (2011). Everything You Need to Know About Open Innovation. Forbes.com

Chesbrough, H., & Bogers, M. (2014). *Explicating Open Innovation: Clarifying an Emerging Paradigm for Understanding Innovation, New Frontiers in Open Innovation*. Oxford: Oxford University Press. https://doi.org/10.1093/acprof.

Chesbrough, H., & Vanhaverbeke, W. (2011). *Open Innovation and Public Policy in Europe*. Research Report. https://doi.org/10.2873/886211.

Clark, H., & Taplin, D. (2012). *Theory of Change Basics: A Primer on Theory of Change, ActKnowledge*. New York: Actknowledge. https://doi.org/10.5327/Z201600010002RBM.

Colombo, M. G., Dell'Era, C., & Frattini, F. (2015). Contribution of Innovation Intermediaries to NPD Process. *R&D Management, 45*, 126–146.

Comstock, D. A., & Lockney, D. (2007). NASA's Legacy of Technology Transfer and Prospects for Future Benefits. In *A Collection of Technical Papers—AIAA Space 2007 Conference* (pp. 2969–2978). https://doi.org/10.2514/6.2007-6283.

Cooke, P. (2001). Regional Innovation Systems, Clusters, and the Knowledge Economy. *Industrial and Corporate Change, 10*, 945–974. https://doi.org/10.1093/icc/10.4.945.

Cooke, P. (2012). Knowledge Economy Spillovers, Proximity, and Specialization. In *Interactive Learning for Innovation* (pp. 100–111). London: Palgrave Macmillan. https://doi.org/10.1057/9780230362420_5.

Cooke, P., Gomez Uranga, M., & Etxebarria, G. (1997). Regional Innovation Systems: Institutional and Organisational Dimensions. *Research Policy, 26*, 475–491. https://doi.org/10.1016/S0048-7333(97)00025-5.

Crossan, M. M., Lane, H. W., & White, R. E. (1999). An Organizational Learning Framework: From Intuition to Institution. *The Academy of Management Review, 24*, 522. https://doi.org/10.2307/259140.

Dalziel, M. (2010). Why Do Innovation Intermediaries Exist? In *Druid 2010: Opening Up Innovation: Strategy, Organization and Technology* (p. 23). London: Imperial College London Business School.

Datta, L. (1997). Multimethod Evaluations: Using Case Studies Together with Other Methods. In W. R. Shadish & E. Chelimsky (Eds.), *Evaluation for the 21st Century: A Handbook* (pp. 344–360). Thousand Oaks: Sage.

De Solla Price, D. (1963). *Big Science, Little Science.* New York: Columbia University.

Dell'Era, C., & Landoni, P. (2014). Living Lab: A Methodology Between User-Centred Design and Participatory Design. *Creativity and Innovation Management, 23*, 137–154. https://doi.org/10.1111/caim.12061.

Deschamps, I., Macedo, M. G., & Eve-Levesque, C. (2013). University-SME Collaboration and Open Innovation: Intellectual-Property Management Tools and the Roles of Intermediaries. *Technology Innovation and Management Review, 3*, 33–41.

Doh, S., & Kim, B. (2014). Government Support for SME Innovations in the Regional Industries: The Case of Government Financial Support Program in South Korea. *Research Policy, 43*, 1557–1569. https://doi.org/10.1016/J.RESPOL.2014.05.001.

Dosi, G., Malerba, F., Ramello, G. B., & Silva, F. (2006). Information, Appropriability, and the Generation of Innovative Knowledge Four Decades After Arrow and Nelson: An Introduction. *Industrial and Corporate Change, 15*, 891–901. https://doi.org/10.1093/icc/dtl028.

Duff, A. (1996). Best Practice in Business Incubator Management. Booragoon: AUSTEP Strategic Partnering.

Edler, J., Cunningham, P., Gök, A., & Shapira, P. (2013). Impacts of Innovation Policy: Synthesis and Conclusions. (Report prepared as part of the project "Compendium of Evidence on the Effectiveness of Innovation Policy Intervention." (NESTA)). Manchester: Manchester Institute of Innovation Research.

Edquist, C. (2004). Reflections on the Systems of Innovation Approach. *Science and Public Policy, 31*, 485–489.

Edwards, T. (2000). Innovation and Organizational Change: Developments Towards an Interactive Process Perspective. *Technology Analysis & Strategic Management, 12*, 445–464. https://doi.org/10.1080/713698496.

Edwards, T., Delbridge, R., & Munday, M. (2005). Understanding Innovation in Small and Medium-Sized Enterprise: A Process Manifest. *Technovation, 25*, 1119–1127.

Eriksson, M., Niitamo, V., Kulkki, S., & Hribernik, K. A. (2006). Living Labs as a Multi-Contextual R & D Methodology. In *The 12th International Conference on Concurrent Enterprising: Innovative Products and Services Through Collaborative Networks* (pp. 26–28). ICE. https://doi.org/10.1109/ICE.2006.7477082.

ESA. (2019). UKube-1 (United Kingdom Universal Bus Experiment 1) [WWW Document]. eoPortal Dir. https://earth.esa.int/web/eoportal/satellite-missions/u/ukube-1. Accessed 10 May 2019.

Esparza, J., & Yamada, T. (2007). The Discovery Value of "Big Science". *The Journal of Experimental Medicine, 204*, 701–704. https://doi.org/10.1084/jem.20070073.

European Commission. (2014). *Regional Research and Innovation Strategies for Smart Specialisation (RIS3)*. Brussels.

Farole, T., Rodríguez-Pose, A., & Storper, M. (2010). Human Geography and the Institutions That Underlie Economic Growth. *Progress in Human Geography, 35*, 58–80. https://doi.org/10.1177/0309132510372005.

Ferraro, P. J. (2009). Counterfactual Thinking and Impact Evaluation in Environmental Policy. *New Directions for Evaluation, 2009*, 75–84. https://doi.org/10.1002/ev.297.

Feurstein, K., Hesmer, A., Hribernik, K. A., Thoben, K. D., & Schumacher, J. (2008). Living Labs: A New Development Strategy. In *European Living Labs-a New Approach for Human Centric Regional Innovation*. Berlin: Wissenschaftlicher Verlag.

Flanagan, K., Uyarra, E., & Laranja, M. (2011). Reconceptualising the 'Policy Mix' for Innovation. *Research Policy, 40*, 702–713. https://doi.org/10.1016/j.respol.2011.02.005.

Fleck, J. (1993). Innofusion: Feedback in the Innovation Process. In *Systems Science* (pp. 169–174). Boston: Springer. https://doi.org/10.1007/978-1-4615-2862-3_30.

Følstad, A. (2008). Living Labs for Innovation and Development of Information and Communication Technology: A Literature Review. *The Electronic Journal for Virtual Organizations and Networks, 10*, 99–131.

Freeman, C. (1991). Networks of Innovators: A Synthesis of Research Issues. *Research Policy, 20*, 499–514. https://doi.org/10.1016/0048-7333(91)90072-X.

Freeman, R. H. (2020). Overview: Satellite Constellations. *Journal of Space Operations & Communicator, 17*(2).

Frenz, M., & Oughton, C. (2005). Innovation in the UK Regions and Devolved Administrations: A Review of the Literature. In *Final Report for the Department of Trade and ....* London: Department for Trade and Industry.

Fuchs, E. (2009). *The Role of DARPA in Seeding and Encourage New Technology Trajectories.* Sloan Industry Studies Working Papers 2001–2009.

Gallison, P., & Hevly, B. (1992). *Big Science: The Growth of Large-Scale Research.* New York: Stanford University Press.

Genta, G., & Rycroft, M. (2003). *Space, the Final Frontier?* Cambridge: Cambridge University Press.

Georghiou, L. (1993). National Systems of Innovation. In B.-A. Lundvall (Ed.), *Towards a Theory of Innovation and Interactive Learning* (Pinter Publishers, London. 1992, pp. xiii + 342, £45, ISBN 1-85567-063-1, Prometheus). London: Pinter. https://doi.org/10.1080/08109029308629360.

Green, K., Hull, R., Mcmeekin, A., & Walsh, V. (1999). The Construction of the Techno-Economic: Networks Vs. Paradigms. *Research Policy, 28*, 777–792.

Grindley, P., Mowery, D. C., & Silverman, B. (1994). SEMATECH and Collaborative Research: Lessons in the Design of High-Technology Consortia. *Journal of Policy Analysis and Management, 13*, 723. https://doi.org/10.2307/3325495.

Gross, R., Blyth, W., & Heptonstall, P. (2010). Risks, Revenues and Investment in Electricity Generation: Why Policy Needs to Look Beyond Costs. *Energy Economics*. https://doi.org/10.1016/j.eneco.2009.09.017.

Hackett, S. M., & Dilts, D. M. (2004). A Systematic Review of Business Incubation Research. *The Journal of Technology Transfer, 29*, 55–82. https://doi.org/10.1023/B:JOTT.0000011181.11952.0f.

Hakkarainen, L., & Hyysalo, S. (2016). The Evolution of Intermediary Activities: Broadening the Concept of Facilitation in Living Labs. *Technology Innovation Management Review, 6*, 45–58.

Hanley, A., Liu, W. H., & Vaona, A. (2015). Credit Depth, Government Intervention and Innovation in China: Evidence from the Provincial Data. *Eurasian Business Review, 5*, 73–98. https://doi.org/10.1007/s40821-015-0016-2.

Hannon, M. J., Skea, J., & Rhodes, A. (2014). Facilitating and Coordinating UK Energy Innovation Through Systemic Innovation Intermediaries. In *International Conference on Sustainability Transitions* (pp. 27–29).

Hargreaves, T., Hielscher, S., Seyfang, G., & Smith, A. (2012). Exploring the Roles of Intermediaries in UK Community Energy: Grassroots Innovations and Niche Development. *Science, Society & Sustainability, 23*, 1–26.

Heikkinen, M. T., Mainela, T., Still, J., & Tähtinen, J. (2007). Roles for Managing in Mobile Service Development Nets. *Industrial Marketing Management, 36*, 909–925. https://doi.org/10.1016/j.indmarman.2007.05.014.

Heilbron, J. L., & Seidel, R. W. (1989). *Lawrence and His Laboratory: A History of the Lawrence Berkeley Laboratory*. https://doi.org/10.1088/0004-637X/710/1/634.

Hekkert, M. P., Suurs, R. A. A., Negro, S. O., Kuhlmann, S., & Smits, R. E. H. M. (2007). Functions of Innovation Systems: A New Approach for Analysing Technological Change. *Technological Forecasting and Social Change, 74*, 413–432. https://doi.org/10.1016/j.techfore.2006.03.002.

Helfat, C. E., & Quinn, J. B. (2006). *Open Innovation: The New Imperative for Creating and Profiting from TechnologyOpen Innovation: The New Imperative for Creating and Profiting from Technology By Chesbrough Henry*. Boston: Harvard Business School Press, 2003. 227 pages, Hard Cover, $35.00, Academy of Management Perspectives. https://doi.org/10.5465/amp.2006.20591014.

Hinloopen, J. (2004). The Market for Knowledge Brokers. *Small Business Economics, 22*, 407–415. https://doi.org/10.1023/B:SBEJ.0000022210.10016.28.

HM Government. (2017). *Industrial Strategy: Building a Britain Fit for the Future*. London.

Hossain, M. (2017). Technological Forecasting & Social Change Motivations, Challenges, and Opportunities of Successful Solvers on an Innovation Intermediary Platform. *Technological Forecasting and Social Change*. https://doi.org/10.1109/ICEOE.2011.6013395.

Hossain, M., & Kauranen, I. (2016). Open Innovation in SMEs: A Systematic Literature Review. *Journal of Strategy and Management, 9*, 58–73. https://doi.org/10.1108/JSMA-08-2014-0072.

Howells, J. (2006). Intermediation and the Role of Intermediaries in Innovation. *Research Policy, 35*, 715–728. https://doi.org/10.1016/j.respol.2006.03.005.

Hu, Y. (2005). Efficient, High-Quality Force-Directed Graph Drawing. *Mathematica Journal, 10*, 37–71.

Human, S. E., & Provan, K. G. (2000). Legitimacy Building in the Evolution of Small-Firm Multilateral Networks: A Comparative Study of Success and Demise. *Administrative Science Quarterly, 45*, 327. https://doi.org/10.2307/2667074.

Hyysalo, S., & Stewart, J. (2008). Intermediaries, Users and Social Learning in Technological Innovation. *International Journal of Innovation Management, 12*, 295–325. https://doi.org/10.1142/S1363919608002035.

Inkpen, A. C., & Tsang, E. W. K. (2005). Social Capital, Networks, and Knowledge Transfer. *The Academy of Management Review, 30*, 146–165. https://doi.org/10.5465/AMR.2005.15281445.

Iturrioz, C., Aragón, C., & Narvaiza, L. (2015). How to Foster Shared Innovation Within SMEs' Networks: Social Capital and the Role of Intermediaries. *European Management Journal, 33*, 104–115. https://doi.org/10.1016/j.emj.2014.09.003.

Jackson, E. T. (2013). Journal of Sustainable Finance & Interrogating the Theory of Change: Evaluating Impact Investing Where It Matters Most. *Journal of Sustainable Finance & Investment, 3*, 37–41. https://doi.org/10.1080/20430795.2013.776257.

Jacob, M., & Hallonsten, O. (2012). The Persistence of Big Science and Megascience in Research and Innovation Policy. *Science and Public Policy, 39*, 411–415. https://doi.org/10.1093/scipol/scs056.

Katzy, B., Turgut, E., Holzmann, T., & Sailer, K. (2013). Innovation Intermediaries: A Process View on Open Innovation Coordination. *Technology Analysis & Strategic Management, 25*, 295–309. https://doi.org/10.1080/09537325.2013.764982.

Kerry, C., & Danson, M. (2016). Open Innovation, Triple Helix and Regional Innovation Systems. *Industry and Higher Education, 30*, 67–78. https://doi.org/10.5367/ihe.2016.0292.

Kilelu, C. W., Klerkx, L., Leeuwis, C., & Hall, A. (2011). Beyond Knowledge Brokering: An Exploratory Study on Innovation Intermediaries in an Evolving Smallholder Agricultural System in Kenya. *Knowledge Management for Development Journal, 7*, 84–108. https://doi.org/10.1080/19474199.2011.593859.

Kim, E. S. (2015). *Facilitating Innovation in SMEs: The Case of Public Intermediaries in South Korea* [Doctoral Thesis]. Edinburgh: The University of Edinburgh.

Kinsella, W. (1996). A "Fusion" of Interests: Big Science, Government, and Rhetorical Practice in Nuclear Fusion Research. *Rhetoric Society Quarterly, 26*, 65–81. https://doi.org/10.1080/02773949609391079.

Kivimaa, P. (2014). Government-Affiliated Intermediary Organisations as Actors in System-Level Transitions. *Research Policy, 43*, 1370–1380. https://doi.org/10.1016/j.respol.2014.02.007.

Klerkx, L., & Leeuwis, C. (2008). Matching Demand and Supply in the Agricultural Knowledge Infrastructure: Experiences with Innovation Intermediaries. *Food Policy, 33*, 260–276. https://doi.org/10.1016/J.FOODPOL.2007.10.001.

Klerkx, L., Álvarez, R., & Campusano, R. (2015). The Emergence and Functioning of Innovation Intermediaries in Maturing Innovation Systems: The Case of Chile. *Innovation and Development, 5*, 73–91. https://doi.org/10.1080/2157930X.2014.921268.

Klewitz, J., Zeyen, A., & Hansen, E. G. (2013). Intermediaries Driving Eco-Innovation in SMEs: A Qualitative Investigation. *European Journal of Innovation Management, 15*, 442–467. https://doi.org/10.1108/14601061211272376.

Kokshagina, O., & Le Masson, P. (2015). Fast-Connecting Open Innovation Practices: On the Role of Intermediaries to Accelerate the Absorptive Capacity Function. *ISPIM Conference, 120*, 232–239.

Lee, S., Park, G., Yoon, B., & Park, J. (2010). Open Innovation in SMEs-an Intermediated Network Model. *Research Policy, 39*, 290–300. https://doi.org/10.1016/j.respol.2009.12.009.

Leydesdorff, L., & Etzkowitz, H. (1995). The Triple Helix—University-Industry-Government Relations: A Laboratory for Knowledge Base Economics Development. *EASST Review, 14*, 14–19.

Lichtenthaler. (2013). Markets for Technology: The Definition. *Journal of Product Innovation Management, 30*, 1–9.

Lin, H., Zeng, S., Liu, H., & Li, C. (2016). How Do Intermediaries Drive Corporate Innovation? A Moderated Mediating Examination. *Journal of Business Research, 69*, 4831–4836. https://doi.org/10.1016/j.jbusres.2016.04.039.

Löfsten, H., & Lindelöf, P. (2002). Science Parks and the Growth of New Technology-Based Firms—Academic-Industry Links, Innovation and Markets. *Research Policy, 31*, 859–876. https://doi.org/10.1016/S0048-7333(01)00153-6.

London Economics. (2009). *The Case for Space 2009*. London.

London Economics. (2014). *The Size and Health of UK Space Industry*. London.

London Economics. (2015a). *The Case for Space 2015*. London: Economics.

London Economics. (2015b). *Development of the Scottish Space Industry*. Edinburgh.

London Economics. (2016). *The Size and Health of the UK Space Industry 2016*. London.

London Economics. (2019). *Size and Health of the UK Space Industry 2018*. London.

Lopez-Vega, H. (2009). How Demand-Driven Technological Systems of Innovation Work? The Role of Intermediary Organizations. In *DRUID-DIME Academy PhD Conference*.

Love, J. H., & Roper, S. (2015). SME Innovation, Exporting and Growth: A Review of Existing Evidence. *International Small Business Journal, 33*, 28–48. https://doi.org/10.1177/0266242614550190.

Lukkarinen, J., Berg, A., Salo, M., Tainio, P., Alhola, K., & Antikainen, R. (2018). An Intermediary Approach to Technological Innovation Systems (TIS)—The Case of the Cleantech Sector in Finland. In *Environmental Innovation and*

Societal Transitions (pp. 136–146). https://doi.org/10.1016/j.eist.2017.04.003.

Lundvall, B. Å., Johnson, B., Andersen, E. S., & Dalum, B. (2002). National Systems of Production, Innovation and Competence Building. *Research Policy, 31*, 213–231. https://doi.org/10.1016/S0048-7333(01)00137-8.

Macdonald, K. (2017). Scottish Space Industry Soaring High [WWW Document]. *BBC News*. http://www.bbc.co.uk/news/38804310

Macdonald, M. (2019). State of the Scottish Nation's Space Sector. In *Proceedings of NSSC*. Edinburgh.

Macdonald, M., & Lowe, C. J. (2014). It's Hip to Be Square: The CubeSat Revolution. *Aerospace*, 22–25.

Malerba, F. (2002). Sectoral Systems of Innovation and Production. *Research Policy, 31*, 247–264.

Malerba, F. (2004). *Sectoral Systems of Innovation: Concepts, Issues and Analyses of Six Major Sectors in Europe*. Cambridge: Cambridge University Press. https://doi.org/10.1017/CBO9780511493270.

Malerba, F. (2005). Sectoral Systems of Innovation: A Framework for Linking Innovation to the Knowledge Base, Structure and Dynamics of Sectors. *Economics of Innovation and New Technology, 14*, 63–82. https://doi.org/10.1080/1043859042000228688.

Malerba, F., & McKelvey, M. (2020). Knowledge-Intensive Innovative Entrepreneurship Integrating Schumpeter, Evolutionary Economics, and Innovation Systems. *Small Business Economics, 54*, 503–522. https://doi.org/10.1007/s11187-018-0060-2.

Malerba, F., & Orsenigo, L. (1995). Schumpeterian Patterns of Innovation. *Cambridge Journal of Economics, 19*, 47–65. https://doi.org/10.1093/oxfordjournals.cje.a035308.

Malerba, F., Caloghirou, Y., McKelvey, M., & Radoševic, S. (2015). *Dynamics of Knowledge Intensive Entrepreneurship: Business Strategy and Public Policy*. London: Routledge.

Markides, C. C., & Anderson, J. (2006). Creativity Is Not Enough: ICT-Enabled Strategic Innovation. *European Journal of Innovation Management, 9*, 129–148. https://doi.org/10.1108/14601060610663532.

Markman, G. D., Phan, P. H., Balkin, D. B., & Gianiodis, P. T. (2005). Entrepreneurship and University-Based Technology Transfer. *Journal of Business Venturing, 20*, 241–263. https://doi.org/10.1016/j.jbusvent.2003.12.003.

Markman, G. D., Siegel, D. S., & Wright, M. (2008). Research and Technology Commercialization. *Journal of Management Studies, 45*, 1401–1423. https://doi.org/10.1111/j.1467-6486.2008.00803.x.

Martin, S., & Scott, J. T. J. T. (2000). The Nature of Innovation Market Failure and the Design of Public Support for Private Innovation. *Research Policy, 29*, 437–447. https://doi.org/10.1016/S0048-7333(99)00084-0.

Mazzoleni, R., & Nelson, R. R. (2007). Public Research Institutions and Economic Catch-Up. *Research Policy, 36*, 1512–1528. https://doi.org/10.1016/j.respol.2007.06.007.

Mazzucato, M., & Penna, C. C. R. (2016). Beyond Market Failures: The Market Creating and Shaping Roles of State Investment Banks. *Journal of Economic Policy Reform, 19*, 305–326. https://doi.org/10.1080/17487870.2016.1216416.

McEvily, B., & Zaheer, A. (1999). Bridging Ties: A Source of Firm Heterogeneity in Competitive Capabilities. *Strategic Management Journal, 20*, 1133–1156. https://doi.org/10.1002/(SICI)1097-0266(199912)20:12<1133::AID-SMJ74>3.0.CO;2-7.

Mgumia, A. H., Mattee, A. Z., & Kundi, B. A. T. (2015). Contribution of Innovation Intermediaries in Agricultural Innovation: The Case of Agricultural R&D in Tanzania. *African Journal of Science, Technology, Innovation and Development, 7*, 151–160. https://doi.org/10.1080/20421338.2015.1023644.

Mian, S. (1996). Assessing Value-Added Contributions of University Technology Business Incubators to. Tenant Firms'. *Research Policy, 25*, 325–335.

Neffke, F., Hartog, M., Boschma, R., & Henning, M. (2014). *The Role of Firms and Entrepreneurs in Regional Diversification*. Utrecht: Utrecht University, Section of Economic Geography.

Nelson, R. R. (1959). The Simple Economics of Basic Scientific Research. *Journal of Political Economy, 67*, 297–306. https://doi.org/10.1086/258177.

Nelson, R. R. (1993). *National Innovation Systems: A Comparative Analysis*. University of Illinois at Urbana-Champaign's Academy for Entrepreneurial Leadership Historical Research Reference in Entrepreneurship. Champaign, IL: University of Illinois.

Ngwenya, H., & Hagmann, J. (2011). Making Innovation Systems Work in Practice: Experiences in Integrating Innovation, Social Learning and Knowledge in Innovation Platforms. *Knowledge Management for Development Journal, 7*, 109–124. https://doi.org/10.1080/19474199.2011.593867.

Nilsson, M., & Sia-Ljungström, C. (2013, February 18–23). The Role of Innovation Intermediaries in Innovation Systems. In *2013 International European Forum* (pp. 161–180). Innsbruck/Igls: International European Forum on System Dynamics and Innovation in Food Networks.

Nishimura, J., & Okamuro, H. (2011). Subsidy and Networking: The Effects of Direct and Indirect Support Programs of the Cluster Policy. *Research Policy, 40*, 714–727. https://doi.org/10.1016/J.RESPOL.2011.01.011.

Nonaka, I., Reinmoeller, P., & Senoo, D. (1998). The "ART" of Knowledge: Systems to Capitalize on Market Knowledge. *European Management Journal, 16*, 673–684. https://doi.org/10.1016/S0263-2373(98)00044-9.

Nutley, S. M., Walter, I., & Davies, H. T. O. (2007). *Using Evidence: How Research Can Inform Public Services*. London: Policy Press.

Nyström, A. G., Leminen, S., Westerlund, M., & Kortelainen, M. (2014). Actor Roles and Role Patterns Influencing Innovation in Living Labs. *Industrial Marketing Management, 43*, 483–495. https://doi.org/10.1016/j.indmarman.2013.12.016.

OECD. (2007). *The Space Economy at a Glance*. OECD Publishing. https://doi.org/10.1787/9789264040847-en.

OECD/European Commission. (2019). Supporting Entrepreneurship and Innovation in Higher Education in Romania. [Report] Paris: OECD.

Oxford Economics. (2010). *The Size and Health of the UK Space Industry a Report for the UK Space Agency*. London.

Oxford Economics. (2012). *The Size and Health of the UK Space Industry*. London.

Parida, V., Westerberg, M., & Frishammar, J. (2012). Inbound Open Innovation Activities in High-Tech SMEs: The Impact on Innovation Performance. *Journal of Small Business Management, 50*, 283–309. https://doi.org/10.1111/j.1540-627X.2012.00354.x.

Parikh, M. (2001). Knowledge Management Framework for High-Tech Research and Development. *Engineering Management Journal, 13*, 27–34. https://doi.org/10.1080/10429247.2001.11415124.

Pavitt, K. (1991). What Makes Basic Research Economically Useful? *Research Policy, 20*, 109–119. https://doi.org/10.1016/0048-7333(91)90074-Z.

Pavitt, K. (2003). *The Process of Innovation*. SPRU Working Paper Series, SPRU—Science Policy Research Unit, University of Sussex Business School.

Pavitt, K. (2006). Innovation Processes. In J. Fagerberg, D. C. Mowery, & R. R. Nelson (Eds.), *The Oxford Handbook of Innovation*. Oxford: Oxford University Press.

Petroni, G., Verbano, C., Bigliardi, B., & Galati, F. (2013). Strategies and Determinants for Successful Space Technology Transfer. *Space Policy, 29*, 251–257. https://doi.org/10.1016/j.spacepol.2013.06.010.

Phan, P. H., Siegel, D. S., & Wright, M. (2005). Science Parks and Incubators: Observations, Synthesis and Future Research. *Journal of Business Venturing, 20*, 165–182. https://doi.org/10.1016/j.jbusvent.2003.12.001.

Pittaway, L., Robertson, M., Munir, K., Denyer, D., & Neely, A. (2004). Networking and Innovation: A Systematic Review of the Evidence. *International Journal of Management Reviews, 5–6*, 137–168.

Power, M. (2000). The Audit Society—Second Thoughts. *International Journal of Auditing, 4*, 111–119.

Pullen, A. J. J. J., De Weerd-Nederhof, P. C., Groen, A. J., & Fisscher, O. A. M. M. (2012). Open Innovation in Practice: Goal Complementarity and Closed NPD Networks to Explain Differences in Innovation Performance for SMEs in the Medical Devices Sector. *Journal of Product Innovation Management, 29*, 917–934. https://doi.org/10.1111/j.1540-5885.2012.00973.x.

Radosevic, S. (2017). Assessing EU Smart Specialisation Policy in a Comparative Perspective. In S. Radosevic, A. Curaj, L. Andreescu, & R. Gheorgiu (Eds.), *Advances in the Theory and Practice of Smart Specialization*. London: Elsevier.

Radosevic, S., & Myrzakhmet, M. (2009). Between Vision and Reality: Promoting Innovation Through Technoparks in an Emerging Economy. *Technovation, 29*, 645–656. https://doi.org/10.1016/J.TECHNOVATION.2009.04.001.

Randhawa, K., Josserand, E., Schweitzer, J., & Logue, D. (2017). Knowledge Collaboration Between Organizations and Online Communities: The Role of Open Innovation Intermediaries. *Journal of Knowledge Management, 21*, 1293–1318. https://doi.org/10.1108/JKM-09-2016-0423.

Regulation (EC) No 1059/2003 of the European Parliament and of the Council of 26 May 2003 on the Establishment of a Common Classification of Territorial Units for Statistics (NUTS). (2018). European Parliament, Brussels.

Rossi, P., Lipsey, M., & Freeman, H. (2003). *Evaluation: A Systematic Approach* (7th ed.). London: Sage.

Russo, M., & Rossi, F. (2009). Cooperation Networks and Innovation: A Complex Systems Perspective to the Analysis and Evaluation of a Regional Innovation Policy Programme. *Evaluation, 15*, 75–99. https://doi.org/10.1177/1356389008097872.

Salter, A. J., & Martin, B. R. (2001). The Economic Benefits of Publicly Funded Basic Research: A Critical Review. *Research Policy, 30*, 509–532. https://doi.org/10.1016/S0048-7333(00)00091-3.

Sapsed, J., Grantham, A., & De Fillippi, R. (2007). A Bridge Over Troubled Waters: Bridging Organizations and Entrepreneurial Opportunities in Emerging Sectors. *Research Policy, 36*, 1314.

Satellite Applications Catapult. (2014). *Satellites: The Big Picture*. Harwell.

Satellite Applications Catapult. (2019). Scottish Space Incubation Programme [WWW Document]. https://sa.catapult.org.uk/opportunities/scottish-space-incubation-programme/. Accessed 31 Mar 2019.

Scarrà, D., & Piccaluga, A. (2020). The Impact of Technology Transfer and Knowledge Spillover from Big Science: A Literature Review. *Technovation*, 102165. https://doi.org/10.1016/j.technovation.2020.102165.

Scottish Enterprise. (2016). Aerospace, Defence, Marine and Security: Industrial Strategy for Scotland 2016. Edinburgh: Scottish Enterprise.

Scottish Enterprise. (2019). SMART: SCOTLAND Grant for SMEs [WWW Document]. https://www.scottish-enterprise.com/support-for-businesses/

funding-and-grants/growing-your-business/smart-scotland-grant. Accessed 6 May 2019.

Siegel, D. S., Waldman, D., & Link, A. (2003). Assessing the Impact of Organizational Practices on the Relative Productivity of University Technology Transfer Offices: An Exploratory Study. *Research Policy, 32*, 27–48. https://doi.org/10.1016/S0048-7333(01)00196-2.

Simard, C., & West, J. (2006). Knowledge networks and the geographic locus of innovation. In: Chesbrough, H., Vanhaverbeke, W., & West, J. (Eds.). (2006). *Open innovation: Researching a new paradigm*. Oxford: Oxford University Press. pp. 220–240.

Smits, R., & Kuhlmann, S. (2004). The Rise of Systemic Instruments in Innovation Policy. *International Journal of Foresight and Innovation Policy, 1*, 4. https://doi.org/10.1504/IJFIP.2004.004621.

Space IGS. (2011). The Space Innovation and Growth Strategy: Main Report.

Space IGS. (2014). Space Growth Action Plan.

Space Network Scotland. (2017). Organisational Support for the Space Sector in Scotland [WWW Document]. https://www.space-network.scot/blog/support-for-the-space-sector.html. Accessed 10 May 2019.

Stare, M., Bucar, M., & Udovic, B. (2014). Soustvarjanje znanja med javnimi raziskovalnimi organizacijami in gospodarstvom za povecanje konkurencnosti. *IB Revija, 3–4*, 53–59.

STFC. (2013). Higgs Theory 'Gains' Mass! [WWW Document]. https://www.stfc.ac.uk/2960.aspx

STFC. (2018). Higgs Centre for Innovation. https://www.roe.ac.uk/higgscentre/

Stojčić, N., & Aralica, Z. (2018). (De)Industrialisation and Lessons for Industrial Policy in Central and Eastern Europe. *Post-Communist Economies, 30*, 713–734. https://doi.org/10.1080/14631377.2018.1443251.

Sun, P. Y. T., & Anderson, M. H. (2010). An Examination of the Relationship Between Absorptive Capacity and Organizational Learning, and a Proposed Integration. *International Journal of Management Reviews, 12*, 130–150. https://doi.org/10.1111/j.1468-2370.2008.00256.x.

Swann, G. M. P. (2009). *The Economics of Innovation: An Introduction, 2009*. New York: Edward Elgar Publishing. https://doi.org/10.1556/AOecon.60.2010.4.6.

Thérin, F. (2007). *Handbook of Research on Techno-Entrepreneurship*. New York: Elgar Edward Publishing.

Tidd, J., Bessant, J., & Pavitt, K. (2005). *Managing Innovation: Integrating Technological, Managerial Organizational Change* (3rd ed.). New York: John Wiley and Sons.

Tontine. (2018). Join Tontine's Space UK Incubator Programme [WWW Document]. https://www.tontineglasgow.co.uk/Blogs/ViewBlog/36. Accessed 11 May 2019.

Tsujimoto, M., Kajikawa, Y., Tomita, J., & Matsumoto, Y. (2018). A Review of the Ecosystem Concept—Towards Coherent Ecosystem Design. *Technological Forecasting and Social Change, 136*, 49–58. https://doi.org/10.1016/j.techfore.2017.06.032.

Tullock, G., Brady, G., & Seldon, A. (2002). Government Failure: A Primer in Public Choice. Washington, D.C.: Cato Institute.

UK Space Agency. (2014a). *Government Response to the UK Space Innovation and Growth Strategy 2014–2030.* Space Growth Action Plan. Swindon: UK Space Agency.

UK Space Agency. (2014b). UKube-1—Case Study [WWW Document]. Gov.UK. https://www.gov.uk/government/case-studies/ukube-1. Accessed 10 May 2019.

UK Space Agency. (2015). UKube-1 Completes Mission [WWW Document]. Gov.UK. https://www.gov.uk/government/news/ukube-1-completes-mission. Accessed 10 May 2019.

UK Space Agency. (2017). New Business Incubators Will Help Space Industry Grow. https://www.gov.uk/government/news/new-business-incubators-will-help-space-industry-grow#:~:text=The%20UK%20Space%20Agency%20has,space%20sector%20across%20the%20UK.&text=The%20University%20of%20Leicester%20will,help%20students%20develop%20entrepreneurial%20ideas.

UK Space Agency. (2019). The Wider Benefits of Space Investments for the UK Economy. https://www.gov.uk/government/news/the-wider-benefits-of-space-investments-for-the-uk-economy#:~:text=Investments%20in%20space%20programmes%20bring,society%2C%20a%20new%20report%20shows.&text=Every%20%C2%A31%20of%20public,benefits%20to%20the%20UK%20economy.

University of Wisconsin-Madison. (2020). Logic Models—Program Development and Evaluation [WWW Document]. https://fyi.extension.wisc.edu/programdevelopment/logic-models/. Accessed 6 July 2020.

Valdaliso, J. M., Magro, E., Navarro, M., Aranguren, M. J., & Wilson, J. R. (2014). Path Dependence in Policies Supporting Smart Specialisation Strategies Insights from the Basque Case. *European Journal of Innovation Management, 17*, 390–408. https://doi.org/10.1108/EJIM-12-2013-0136.

Vallejo, B., Oyelaran-Oyeyinka, B., Ozor, N., & Bolo, M. (2019). Open Innovation and Innovation Intermediaries in Sub-Saharan Africa. *Sustainability, 11*, 392. https://doi.org/10.3390/su11020392.

van de Vrande, V., De Jong, J., Vanhaverbeke, W., & de Rochemont, M. (2009). Open Innovation in SMEs: Trends, Motives and Management Challenges. *Technovation, 29*, 423–437. https://doi.org/10.1016/j.technovation.2008.10.001.

Van der Meulen, B., Nedeva, M., Braun, D., van der Meulen, B., Nedeva, M., & Braun, D. (2005). *Intermediaries Organisation and Processes: Theory and Research Issues.* PRIME Workshop.

Vass, S. (2013). SE Aims to Help Scots Space Firms Conquer the Final Frontier: Winning Funding. *Herald*.

Venturini, K., & Verbano, C. (2014). A Systematic Review of the Space Technology Transfer Literature: Research Synthesis and Emerging Gaps. *Space Policy, 30*, 98–114. https://doi.org/10.1016/j.spacepol.2014.04.003.

Vidmar, M. (2019a). *Scottish Space Sector and Innovation a PERIpatetic Study of an Emerging Innovation System and the Roles of Innovation Intermediaries*. Edinburgh: The University of Edinburgh.

Vidmar, M. (2019c). The Ten Million Euro Question: How Do Innovation Intermediaries Support Smart Specialization? *Croatian Economic Survey, 21*, 37–84.

Vidmar, M. (2019d). Agile Space Living Lab—The Emergence of a New High-Tech Innovation Paradigm. *Space Policy, 49*, 101324.

Vidmar, M. (2019e). *The "Living Lab" Method: Discovery > Challenge > Innovation*. Edinburgh. https://doi.org/10.13140/RG.2.2.21744.20484.

Vidmar, M. (2020). New Space and Innovation Policy: Scotland's Emerging "Space Glen". *New Space, 8*, 31–51. https://doi.org/10.1089/space.2019.0032.

Vidmar, M. (2021). Enablers, Equippers, Shapers and Movers: A typology of innovation intermediaries interventions and the development of an emergent innovation system. *Acta Astronautica, 179*, 280–289.

Vidmar, M., Golra, O., & Rosiello, A., (2020). Resilience of New Space Firms in the UK During the Early Stages of Covid-19 Crisis: The Case for Strategic Agility. *New Space, 8*(4).

Vidmar, M., Rosiello, A., Williams, R., Vermeulen, N., & Dines, J. (2020b). New Space and Agile Innovation: Understanding Transition to Open Innovation Through Examining Innovation Networks and Moments. *Acta Astronautica, 167*, 122–134.

Von Tunzelmann, N. (2009). Competencies Versus Capabilities: A Reassessment. *Economics and Politics, 26*, 435–464. https://doi.org/10.1428/30999.

Vonortas, N. S. (2002). Building Competitive Firms: Technology Policy Initiatives in Latin America. *Technology in Society, 24*, 433–459. https://doi.org/10.1016/S0160-791X(02)00034-9.

Wang, J. (2018). Innovation and Government Intervention: A Comparison of Singapore and Hong Kong. *Research Policy, 47*, 399–412. https://doi.org/10.1016/j.respol.2017.12.008.

Weinberg, A. M. (1961). Impact of Large-Scale Science on the United States. *Science, 134*, 161–164. https://doi.org/10.1126/science.134.3473.161.

West, J., & Bogers, M. (2014). Leveraging External Sources of Innovation: A Review of Research on Open Innovation. *Journal of Product Innovation Management, 31*, 814–831. https://doi.org/10.1111/jpim.12125.

West, J., Salter, A., Vanhaverbek, W., & Chesbrough, H. (2014). Open Innovation: The Next Decade. *Research Policy, 43*, 805–811. https://doi.org/10.1016/J.RESPOL.2014.03.001.

Willetts, D. (2013). *8 Great Technologies, 2013*. London: Policy Exchange.

Winch, G. M., & Courtney, R. (2007). The Organization of Innovation Brokers: An International Review. *Technology Analysis & Strategic Management, 19*, 747–763. https://doi.org/10.1080/09537320701711223.

Wright, M., Roper, S., Hart, M., & Carter, S. (2015). Joining the Dots: Building the Evidence Base for SME Growth Policy. *International Small Business Journal, 33*, 3–11. https://doi.org/10.1177/0266242614558316.

Zahra, S. A., & George, G. (2002). Absorptive Capacity: A Review, Reconceptualization, and Extension. *The Academy of Management Review, 27*, 185–203. https://doi.org/10.5465/AMR.2002.6587995.

Zuijdam, F., Boekholt, P., Deuten, J., Meijer, I., & Vermeulen, N. (2011). *The Role and Added Value of Large-Scale Research Facilities*. Amsterdam: Technopolis Group.

Index[1]

[1] Note: Page numbers followed by 'n' refer to notes.

M. Vidmar, *Innovation Intermediaries and (Final) Frontiers of High-tech*, https://doi.org/10.1007/978-3-030-60642-8